PRAISE FOR *DRIVE*

"Kelley's extraordinary experiences have helped shape her into one of the most sincere, down-to-earth, and honest people I've encountered in both business and life. With incredible candor and relatability, she takes readers inside her unique journey and shares a remarkable leadership style that's all her own. Built on integrity, compassion, and the Earnhardt family's trademark drive to succeed, Kelley's story serves as a road map for servant leadership and putting people first."
—Rick Hendrick
   Owner of Hendrick Motorsports; chairman and
   CEO of Hendrick Automotive Group

"Kelley masterfully shares complex subject matter in a personal and easily understandable way in *Drive*. The look into Kelley and Dale's childhood and her journey to become one of the most influential female executives in all of sports is an inspiration to all. The 'lessons learned' portion of the book only confirms why I have always looked up to Kelley. This is a great read not only for NASCAR fans but for those who want to be better leaders, parents, and human beings."
—Jim McCoy
   Vice president, Nationwide Marketing

"Kelley Earnhardt Miller is an incredible mix of hard-nosed business sense, creativity, and loyalty. While being a great businessperson seems effortless to her, she has an uncanny ability to lead a diverse set of employees while racking up wins, growing the company, serving on boards, and raising a family. To get a peek inside her mind is a true privilege for those who want the secrets to her success."
—Thayer Lavielle
   Executive vice president of talent marketing
   and operations, The Collective

"It is a rare thing to find a book that is so brilliantly written for business *and* life. Kelley will help you win at both like no one else can—with heart and unmatched experience. As a mom to three and CEO of a dynamic business, I found that *Drive* had a profound effect on how I intentionally pursue what matters. Get ready to be inspired and challenged to take your work and life to the next level—a must-read!"
—Lara Casey
   CEO of Cultivate What Matters;
   author of *Cultivate* and *Make It Happen*

"Kelley finds a way to drop the curtain surrounding what some might call insider knowledge about the sport of NASCAR and the business that fuels it. But even more impressive is the way she also drops the same curtain when it comes to herself. Her honesty and vulnerability make this book not only a great read but an important work/life handbook."

—Krista Voda Kelley
Television host; reporter for NASCAR on NBC

"Reading Kelley's *Drive* felt like sitting in a room and listening to her tell me all the things she addresses directly and only to me. Through this book, you not only get sage advice from someone who has made a name for herself; you also get to know Kelley. You learn why those who know her respect and appreciate her."

—Mike Helton
Vice chairman of NASCAR

"The impact of the Earnhardt family in my life and career has been immeasurable. I've practically watched Kelley Earnhardt Miller grow from that confident little girl hanging out with her dad and brother at the racetrack in the early eighties to a successful businesswoman today. Kelley is a person of utmost integrity and has a work ethic like none other. As a result of that hardworking attitude, I'm confident that this book will succeed. Kelley is not only a special friend to the Childresses, but I consider her to be a part of our family."

—Richard Childress
Chairman and CEO of Richard Childress Racing

"I got to know Kelley when my team put together the deal for me to come to JR Motorsports and make the move to NASCAR. I've always respected the way that Kelley works to be the best leader for her team, not just the best female leader. She's a strong woman in a man's world who has helped pave the way for other women in the industry. Kelley expects the best out of her employees, and she pushes those around her to succeed."

—Danica Patrick
Former professional racecar driver

"Be ready to be inspired. The genuine character and professional excellence that define who Kelley is will guide you to becoming a better person. Enjoy learning about my friend and what she values in her life, which will likely lift you to another level."

—Ryan Newman
NASCAR Monster Energy Cup Series driver for Roush Fenway Racing

"Practical lessons and easy to understand! The honest and humble way Kelley shares her personal experiences and lessons learned is remarkably simple. This is a great book for anyone wanting to be successful in business while protecting what's really important: their family relationships."

—Scott Hunt
CEO of Hunt Brothers Pizza

"Through the great sport of fishing I have been very blessed to have come to know many extraordinary people from all walks of life. I have fished with presidents, prime ministers, leaders of industries, and people in the conservation world. Of all the people, including some real characters, I would place Dale Earnhardt Sr. right up at the top of the list of truly remarkable individuals. In many ways, Kelley is a chip off the ol' block. Just like her dad and famous brother, she is one of my heroes. She has the same Earnhardt savvy, drive, fire in the belly, and determination but just happens to be a little—or maybe a lot—more organized. Thanks, Kelley, for sharing your inspirational life story with no holds barred. I love you, and I love this book!"

—Johnny Morris
Founder, Bass Pro Shops

"A true conglomeration of feeling, emotion, wisdom, experience, life, family, business, success, challenge, setback, victory, and legacy! Kelley opens her heart and transforms her personal demons, trials, and tribulations, as well as experience and triumphs, into positive lessons and challenges for the rest of us to garner. Kelley has revealed the paradigm of courage, wisdom, and beauty that she truly is, both inside and out, and presented it in typical, heartfelt Earnhardt fashion to win and help others win as well."

—Rick Brandt
President and CEO, Brandt, Inc.

"*Drive* is an amazing insight into the personal and professional mind of one of the most well-respected leaders in our NASCAR garage. Not only did I learn things about the Earnhardt family growing up, but I learned how to make better decisions in my life at home and in my business ventures. *Drive* is a must-read for everyone wanting to follow their dreams in life, both personal and professional!"

—Sherry Pollex
Vice president and founder of the Martin Truex Jr. Foundation and SherryStrong.org

DRIVE

9 LESSONS TO WIN

IN BUSINESS AND IN LIFE

KELLEY EARNHARDT MILLER

WITH BETH CLARK

W Publishing Group

An Imprint of Thomas Nelson

Published in Nashville, Tennessee, by W Publishing, an imprint of Thomas Nelson.

Thomas Nelson titles may be purchased in bulk for educational, business, fund-raising, or sales promotional use. For information, please e-mail SpecialMarkets@ ThomasNelson.com.

Any Internet addresses, phone numbers, or company or product information printed in this book are offered as a resource and are not intended in any way to be or to imply an endorsement by Thomas Nelson, nor does Thomas Nelson vouch for the existence, content, or services of these sites, phone numbers, companies, or products beyond the life of this book.

ISBN 978-0-7852-2935-3 (eBook)
ISBN 978-0-7852-2930-8 (HC)

Library of Congress Cataloging-in-Publication Data

Library of Congress Control Number: 2019952389

Printed in the United States of America

20 21 22 23 24 LSC 10 9 8 7 6 5 4 3 2 1

To my husband, L.W., who is always my voice of reason and my fierce protector. Though he questioned whether I needed to take on another project, he believed in me, supported me, and encouraged me as I tackled this book. He is part of the "how and why" I have grown in my personal life to the point that I can offer wisdom and advice to others as they grow too. L.W., I love you with all my heart and soul. You make me smile.

To my brother, Dale Jr., who has always believed I was the smartest, most capable person on the planet, next to our dad. With that belief, I have been able to manage his business empire, help him achieve success, and gain the business experience and knowledge I am fortunate to share in this book.

To Dr. Karen and Dr. Nicole, who gave me a place to talk, cry, and work through the baggage I carried for so many years. I will be forever grateful for the countless hours of conversation—and for those still to come—that encourage me to be real and to find my voice, which was silenced for many years. This book would not be possible without the work we have done to peel back layers and heal "little Kelley" and to move me forward.

CONTENTS

CONTENTS

PART 3: WHAT I WISH I'D KNOWN

FOREWORD

I am honored that my sister would ask me to write the foreword to her book. When she began working on it, I knew she was hoping to create something that would inspire others, something that would help people achieve their goals and navigate challenges in life—both personally and professionally.

Then I read the book.

Immediately I realized that what she had written was more than a detailed guide to success in business and in life. It was also a glimpse into the childhood that created some challenges for her. Frankly, I was surprised by Kelley's honesty and transparency. But it filled me with pride and made me even more excited about what you, the reader, would learn.

My sister's journey in life has been rewarding to her, and it has given her much to share with others as she has grown into a successful businesswoman, an amazing mother, and a supportive wife. The reality is that this was, at times, a painful process for her, filled with disappointments and letdowns. She faces these experiences head-on in the first part of the book.

Kelley also carefully details the impact she had on my life. From a very young age, Kelley was my guardian. Throughout both of our lives, she has been a motherly influence on me. She has successfully faced the difficulties of balancing that with also overseeing every single aspect of my professional life. She has carried the mental pressure of managing my business empire, and she has done it better than anyone I could imagine. She has made personal sacrifices along the way, and I will always be grateful for that. I trust her completely.

Kelley has grown and changed so much over the years. She's done the hard work necessary to become who she wants to be today. Even this book is part of that process. All through our lives, she has consistently impressed me. I have long wished for others to understand the dynamic individual my sister is. Her strength to overcome personal challenges is inspiring. Her stern brilliance in her professional life has provided stability and happiness to thousands of others. And while she doesn't climb into a racecar and speed around the track as NASCAR's celebrities do, she is a steady hand and a powerful voice behind the scenes in our sport.

I'm excited for you to know my sister's story and to discover the secrets of her success. She'll be excited about what you learn from it and how it may inspire and help you. After all, that's who Kelley is: always inspiring and always helping.

—Dale Earnhardt Jr.

June 2019

MEET ME AT THE TRACK

My mom said I was literally born at a racetrack. The truth is that she went into labor with me right after one of my dad's races one Saturday night in Concord, North Carolina. His father, Ralph Earnhardt, was there, as was my maternal grandfather, Robert Gee. For some reason, my two grandfathers ended up in a fight, and before it was over, my dad was involved in it too. When he and my mom left the track and went home, she went into labor. I was born at 4:16 p.m. the following Monday.

As the daughter of a NASCAR superstar, my name has always had the power to open doors for me. Though I have long had a personal passion for the sport and working in the industry was a natural fit, I never wanted to ride through my career in the passenger seat of my father's legacy. Certainly, he was a winner on the racetrack. He had seventy-six NASCAR Cup Series wins and seven championship titles to prove it. But I didn't view myself as some kind of automatic winner just because my dad was so successful, nor did I think anything should be handed to me because of my genes. I wanted to work hard and earn every position I ever held. That's the way my dad always wanted it.

When my editor suggested *Drive* as the title of this book, I instantly knew it was perfect. Not only does the word *drive* summarize the sport I have loved and been involved in for as long as I can remember, but it also describes what happens in my heart and mind each day. I'm nothing if not driven! I'm driven to succeed personally and professionally; I'm driven to learn and grow in every possible way; I'm driven to make our company the best it can be, both in terms of competitive racing and in terms of being a great place to work; and I'm driven to make a difference in the world.

Believe it or not, there were times years ago when people referred to me as the best driver in the Earnhardt family, which is quite a compliment. I definitely know how to handle a car at high speeds, and I know what it feels like to thrive on the rush of racing around a track ahead of everyone else. But my days behind the wheel are in the past. Now, I enjoy contributing to NASCAR as an executive. The opportunity to engage in our sport as a business leader is a fulfilling privilege and responsibility. The job has its stresses, as every job does, but it's ideal for me.

In this book, you will read about how my brother, Dale Earnhardt Jr., and I started our company, JR Motorsports (JRM). Though I had been exposed to the business side of NASCAR in many ways before we formed our organization, I had never seen exactly the type of company we wanted to create. I had much to learn in order to position us to succeed.

People are understandably curious about how I came to be a racing executive. I don't have a dramatic story about breaking glass ceilings as a woman in a man's world or climbing the corporate ladder in the realm of professional sports. I was simply born into it, and it has been my world all my life.

One of the questions people ask me most is "What's it like to be a female in a male-dominated sport?" Over the years I have come up with a good answer for interviewers and others who ask, but for a long time I never thought about being a woman in a man's world. I still don't think about it often unless someone asks or something happens to call my attention to it.

In January 2015 I attended the first of what has now become a series of regular meetings at NASCAR headquarters. A couple of times a year, the organization gathers a group of approximately fifty owners and drivers to discuss the state of our sport, address issues and concerns, and inform us of rule changes. We also talk about business matters, competition items, and other things we're considering as our industry moves forward. In that half-day meeting, only three of us were women—executive vice president and chief marketing officer of NASCAR Jill Gregory, owner and driver Jennifer Jo Cobb, and me. Now *that* called my attention to the fact that I am a woman in a man's world!

That day I stopped and thought, *Wow. It's pretty special to be in this place and to represent other women who aspire to be here too.*

Whatever I can do to make it easier for other women to be influential in our industry, in the broader world of professional sports, or in any business or personal endeavor, I am happy to do. But my purpose in this book is not to write to women only. The leadership lessons here are equally valuable and applicable to men.

Whether you are just starting out in business or are a seasoned professional, these nine lessons about winning are the ones I have learned on my own. They've changed the way I lead in business and the way I live my personal life. I share them not as a game plan for greatness but as your fellow traveler on life's journey, a journey that is sometimes difficult, painful, unexpected, or confusing, and sometimes exhilarating and joyful. They are lessons I wish someone had shared with me before I learned them the hard way, which is why I now gladly pass them along to you.

I am not offering them as some sort of blueprint for guaranteed winning. In fact, one of the lessons I have learned is that there is not a blueprint for success. As much as we would like to find a formula to win, winning simply does not work that way. It's more organic than that. The road to success is unique to every person, with many twists, turns, and tweaks, some quite unexpected.

In the language of racing, I've had my share of crashes and cautions in life—and they've taught me a lot. If telling my personal story and writing about what I've learned will spare you some mistakes, save you some heartache, give you a leg up, equip you to be a more effective leader, or help you be happier in your job and in your personal life, then I'll consider this book a success.

Every Monday morning after a race weekend, our shop at JRM is full of dirty cars fresh off the track. Our mechanics and crews begin working immediately to prepare them for the next race. They know exactly what to do to get a car ready for a specific track and weather conditions. They are familiar with each driver, and they tailor every car's setup to its driver's style. They think about how the car needs to grip the track. They adjust the suspension and closely monitor the car's weight and balance for optimum handling; and they complete many other tasks to give the car its best possible chance to win the race. Our team knows exactly how to tweak every element of the car to maximize its driving potential and get a victory for JRM. No detail is too small.

Just like a racecar before it takes to the track, each of us needs a certain amount of fine-tuning. To maximize our potential, we make continual adjustments as we go. We work on ourselves and strive to be better. We look to books, people, and other resources for the information and insights we need to improve the way we think and perform.

I have taken part of the journey to success, and part of it is still ahead of me. I am driving it every single day. I've realized that my passion and purpose can be summarized in five words: *helping people be happy people.*

I've also discovered that one of my priorities is to live with an open mind and to be a continual student. I'm always looking to learn something new, to shift a perspective, to try something different. I hope this book will present you with some new ideas and different ways to pursue what success means to you. The lessons and the stories are more of an invitation than an instruction. My desire is that as you read them, think about them, and see how they could work for you, you will soon find yourself winning in business and in life on a whole new level.

PART ONE

GROWING UP EARNHARDT

Everyone is shaped by their experiences, especially in their formative years. For people who are in positions of influence, much of the vision we cast and the passion we impart to the people around us comes from the events and relationships that affected us early in our lives, both positively and negatively. Before I share the lessons I've learned, I would like to tell part of my story. Without it, I would not be the business leader nor the person I am.

You may have picked up this book because the idea of succeeding at everything you do is appealing to you. Or maybe you would like to learn more about my father and the Earnhardt family. Regardless of the reason, I appreciate your interest. You may read some stories that surprise or even disappoint you. I've been told that people like to keep their heroes on pedestals and that no one wants to read negative comments or stories about celebrities. Though I understand the reasoning behind that, it's been essential for me to face the realities of my past. More than anything, that's what has helped to develop the heart of a winner that is in me today.

As I share the behind-the-scenes details of my life as the daughter of a racing legend, I'm in no way attempting to tarnish my father's image. I simply want to tell a real story. You and your family have one, just as my family and I do. And yours is as important to your personal and professional development as mine has been for me.

ONE

MY STARTING POSITION

Any racing fan knows that starting position matters. Where a car is when the green flag waves can have a huge impact on the outcome of the race. The pole position—the inside of the front row—is most desirable and is usually awarded to the car and driver with the best qualifying time for each race. Among the remaining positions, some are considered better than others. A few are viewed as basically unwinnable, depending on the track. Over the course of a race, all sorts of developments can arise, and a car that holds the lead for almost an entire race can lose at the last minute. That fast-paced unpredictability is part of what makes our sport exciting.

What's true at the racetrack is also true about life: where and how we start matters. Our early days don't have to dictate the rest of our lives, but they do influence and determine much about the way we think and feel, the way we relate to others, the way we approach and solve problems, our work ethic, our likes and dislikes, and our priorities.

To use a racing analogy, I could say I got the green flag in Concord, North Carolina, on August 28, 1972. That's the day I was born to a young, ambitious amateur racecar driver named Dale Earnhardt and his wife, Brenda. My dad was twenty-one years old, and Mom described him as "determined and focused" at that time. "He lived very much in the present," she recalled. "He did everything day by day. He didn't think about next week; he only thought about the next race." My mom supported my dad in every way she could. Reminiscing, she shared, "Dale and I both loved life. We had a lot of fun and made a lot of good memories."[1]

My mom was thrilled to have a baby, and she always said that being a mother came naturally to her. Having been raised in a family with seven siblings, she dreamed of spending her life surrounded by children and the proverbial white picket fence. She hungered for stability the way my dad hungered for adventure.

My paternal grandfather, Ralph Earnhardt—a NASCAR legend—was still living when I was born. When he first started racing, he worked various day jobs, and on the side he raced on dirt tracks to make extra money. By 1953 he had enjoyed enough success on the racetrack to begin racing full-time. My grandfather made a name for himself by keeping his car in the best possible condition in every race, and he won numerous awards during the 1950s and '60s, including the 1956 NASCAR Sportsman championship, which is the equivalent of a NASCAR Xfinity Series championship today.

My grandfather died in 1973, when I was about a year old, of a heart attack while working on parts for someone's car. Legend has it—and some websites report[2]—that my dad found his father dead on the garage floor, midway through working on a car. My aunt Cathy, my father's sister, said, "We have tried to correct the 'drama' about Daddy dying in the shop, but it makes a better story than what actually happened."[3]

In reality, the wife of the man whose car parts my grandfather had serviced that day came to pick them up from him. My grandfather told her he was going into the kitchen, a few steps away from the shop, and would be right back. When he didn't return, she found him deceased on the kitchen floor. Aunt Cathy is right; the true story is not as good as the myth!

Two years after I was born, my brother Dale Jr., to whom I'll refer as simply "Dale" in this book, came along. We've always been close, but back then I had no idea that, more than forty years later, we'd work closely together co-owning JR Motorsports, with me managing the business aspects of his life and career and overseeing his brand. But that's where we are today, and we're both thankful for the opportunity.

Dale and I have an older half brother, Kerry, from our dad's first marriage. Though we never lived in the same house and I didn't meet him until I was thirteen years old and Kerry was sixteen, Dale and I now have a good relationship with him and his family.

I have no memory of my parents as a married couple, nor does Dale. They separated in 1976, when I was four years old, and divorced in 1980. I do remember that they treated each other with civility and got along well most of the time. After their separation, Dale and I lived with our mom. She often worked second- or third-shift jobs, and perhaps my protective nature toward Dale has its roots in those years, when I first stepped into my role as a "mother hen" for him. In many situations, we had only each other to turn to and lean on for support and understanding, and those years became an important bonding period for us.

I felt I needed to compensate for Mom's not being home with us. Relatives stayed with us overnight while she worked, but they were not with us twenty-four hours a day, so I learned to cook and do laundry at an early age. Dale was short and skinny and insecure in certain ways, so I did my best to support him, encourage him, and meet his practical needs.

We saw our dad occasionally. I remember playing T-ball as a child and being so excited because my dad had come to the game. I also remember his taking my cousin and me to his mother's house in his very fast Trans Am. We visited our grandmother Earnhardt often, and Dale and I spent a great deal of time with her, especially after school when Mom worked.

Even though our nuclear family didn't live together and I didn't see my dad as much as I wanted to, Mom created a happy life for us, and I'll always appreciate that.

CHANGING LANES

In 1981, when I was eight years old, tragedy struck Mom, Dale, and me. Early one morning in May, about three weeks before school would be out for the summer, our rented house burned. We were living small paycheck to small paycheck, and money was tight. Suddenly, my mom found herself with no home and no money, unable to provide for two young children.

But things were going well for Dad. He had recently won his first championship, and he had greater financial resources than she did. So she made the heartbreaking decision to send Dale and me to live with him while she moved to her mother's house in Norfolk, Virginia.

Dale and I both felt we had changed lanes. Suddenly, everything was different. All that was familiar had gone up in smoke—not just our house but also our furniture, our photographs, our clothes, our toys, and our favorite things. To say that it was not a happy time for us is an understatement, especially with the loss of our everyday relationship with our mother.

Dad was doing well enough in his racing to afford a nanny to stay with Dale and me full-time. He had been the Rookie of the Year in 1979 and was the NASCAR champion in 1980. When he was away on weekends, Mom came to stay with us, which helped our family feel a bit more solid.

In July 1982, Dad sustained a broken leg in a race at Pocono Raceway. I was surprised to learn that a woman named Teresa had visited him at the hospital after the accident. I knew Teresa. Dad had met her before he and my mom divorced, and he dated her off and on for several years. But since the beginning of 1982, he'd had another girlfriend. Dale and I knew her well, and we'd spent time with her and my dad. At the time of the accident, I assumed Dad was seeing her and that he and Teresa were "off." They were not. They were very much on, and on November 14, 1982, Teresa and Dad married.

Teresa was twenty-four years old, seven years younger than my dad. She had no children of her own and no experience dealing with a ten-year-old and an eight-year-old, much less a traumatized ten- and eight-year-old. As any children would, Dale and I wanted our mom, but because of the fire and her job situation, we had no choice but to live with Dad and Teresa. Being on our own with two newlyweds was not easy for us. We turned to each other whenever we were upset, sad, or confused because we felt our dad was unavailable to us.

Thankfully, Dad made enough money racing to be able to provide for our material needs. In his mind, a father's job was to offer his children food, shelter, and clothing—and he did that for us. Our physical needs were met, but Dale and I both had emotional and relational needs that went unfulfilled for many years. As we grew older, Dad became more and more involved in racing and had less time to be part of our lives. In addition, our relationship with Teresa was difficult.

Dad began to enjoy unprecedented levels of success on the racetrack, and almost before Dale and I knew what was happening, he was famous. He won NASCAR Cup Series championships in 1980, 1986, 1987, 1990, 1991, 1993, and 1994. We were now able to afford things we had never had before, and people in public would say hello to our dad or ask for his autograph.

By then, Dad had earned his nickname, "the Intimidator," and he took it seriously. He was very aggressive on the racetrack, and he didn't mind hitting a bumper to gain an advantage over another car. I've never met a NASCAR fan whose feeling about my dad was neutral; people either loved him or hated him. People who loved his style on the racetrack thought he was magical. People who hated it called him a dirty driver.

We were totally surprised and unprepared for the judgment people had toward our dad, whether it was positive or negative. Sometimes I overheard it. Sometimes people said it directly to us. It was intense—and school was no escape from the pressure. We just wanted to be normal young people, but other students referred to us as "rich" and "spoiled," and acted as though they thought everything in our lives was wonderful.

I quickly learned that when you're the daughter of a celebrity, whether that person is an athlete, a movie star, a rock singer, or a politician, people make many assumptions about you. They think your life is glamorous, fun, and happy all the time. They can even become jealous, wishing they were as "lucky" as you are.

But life as the child of a famous racecar driver was difficult for me. Dad's streak of success started when I was only eight years old. I was hurting because of what had happened in our family. I missed my mom and endured conflict with my stepmother, and like all children, I wanted a real relationship with my dad. Unfortunately, that type of relationship simply wasn't available.

I wanted Dad's attention, not a photo from Victory Lane. I longed for him to sit down to dinner with us, to pick me up from school, to come to my programs and sports events, to be part of my life. I just wanted him to do what parents do. After all, my mom lived six hours away from us and she still found ways to show up and support us when we needed it. Teresa was present in our lives, but she didn't relate to us in a motherly fashion.

Dad's success came with prize money, but it also came with a price. It cost me the father-daughter relationship I hungered for. While I'm proud of my dad's accomplishments on the racetrack, they resulted in great personal pain for me.

During those years, I looked forward to visits with my mom more than anything. She made everything so special! She always asked Dale and me what we wanted for Christmas and gave it to us. But our happy holidays with her were special to us not because of the presents but because we knew she wanted to spend time with us.

On the other hand, we dreaded Christmas with Dad and Teresa. Dad was consumed with racing, and Teresa never seemed interested in us at all. Dale and I laugh now about how we got "memorabilia" at our Christmases with them. Our gifts consisted of airport souvenirs from their travel destinations and even free items from hotels. But our disappointment over holidays with them was not about the gifts; it was because they had no idea who we were and what we liked. When we were with them, we didn't feel known or supported. We didn't feel that we mattered in any meaningful way. I believe this is related to my dad's fundamental belief that a father's job is to meet his family's *material* needs—to make the house payment, pay for the groceries, keep us clothed, and make sure we went to school.

My dad tried to do something really great for me when I was sixteen: he gave me a silver 1987 Chevrolet Monte Carlo SS Fastback. It wasn't brand new, but it was a very nice used car. While I realize many people would have given *anything* for that car, *nothing* about it was cool for a teenage girl. When he gave it to me, I didn't care how many guys would drool over it; I just felt—once again—that he didn't truly know me.

He had no idea how much I needed and wanted him to be part of my world. I would have given up the SS Fastback in a split second—and all the other material goods he provided—just to have some quality time with him, just to hear him say he loved me and felt I was important, or to have him demonstrate genuine interest in me. I was surrounded by teenagers who only dreamed of having such a car, and because of my dad's background and the world in which he lived, he thought it was a really nice gift. Of course I was glad to have my own transportation, but the gift fell flat for me because it did nothing to fill the void in my heart. The absence of a father's love and interest in me affected me deeply, and I spent the next twenty-five years of my life trying to fill that hole.

No matter how fabulous other people thought my life was, the truth is that being the child of a celebrity was not always wonderful. Looking back now, if someone were to ask me about the best thing that happened in my growing-up years, I would say it was the opportunity to be a big sister. Dale was my first best friend and the first person, along with my mom, on the team of my life. We've been through a lot together, and to this day, the two of us have a unique brother-sister relationship.

TWO

BIG SISTER

From the day Dale was born, I've taken seriously my role as his big sister. Our mom told me I loved having a baby brother and wanted to treat Dale like my own little baby from the very start. According to her, I was always eager to help with him and felt a sense of responsibility for him at quite a young age. That became even more true when Mom moved to Virginia, and Dad and Teresa were busy with his racing.

In a YouTube interview about this time in our lives, Dale says:

Kelley really became my caretaker and caregiver. She made sure I wasn't dressed like a fool for school, and she made sure I had money in my pocket for lunch. She made sure I'd done my homework and wasn't going to get in trouble. . . . We had daily chores, and she made sure they were done and I was doing what I was supposed to be doing to keep me out of trouble. She coddled me and really took care of me. Dad wasn't taking care of me. I mean, he was racing and gone, and Teresa was with him. But Kelley was there. Kelley is *the* one who was there with me every day. We had housekeepers, and we had two, three, four different nannies that were around. But I never created a relationship with them. My sister was the one I went to every day, for everything.[1]

According to our mom, when Dale and I were young, I was the one who needed to be entertained, enjoyed having other people around, and didn't like being alone. I wanted to be busy all the time. Dale, on the other hand, was content to spend time playing with his toys and could easily entertain himself. He didn't need company and was more self-sufficient than I was.

Another difference between Dale and me—one that would become significant through our teenage years—is that I was a rule follower and he was not. Dad liked to live by rules, so he and I got along well in that regard. If he said we had to get all As on our report cards at school, I got all As. I did so because he expected me to do it.

I didn't seek accolades or applause for good grades, partly because I was content to meet Dad's expectations but mostly because I didn't like the consequences of failing to meet them. Getting in trouble because of a low grade only amplified what I already felt was missing between Dad and me, so I worked hard to avoid it. I never understood why grades were important to my dad, because he wasn't given to explaining anything. We never had conversations about why making good grades was a good idea, nor did he give me any reason or encouragement to excel in school. He simply said, "Make As." So I made As without understanding why it mattered. All I knew was that it would keep me from getting in trouble—and being in trouble caused me to feel unloved.

My dad never asked me what subjects I liked in school or why I liked them. He didn't know which classes were difficult for me, and he didn't offer to arrange for someone to help me with them. He had no idea who my favorite teachers were, who my friends were, or what caused me to struggle. He wasn't one to hand out prizes or praise when I did well; he simply viewed it as me doing what I was supposed to do.

People might assume that Dale and I started racing when we were very young because were born into a family so strongly identified with NASCAR. We did not. In fact, our dad didn't encourage us to become involved in the sport at all. He certainly didn't push Dale to become a driver. While some fathers are eager for their sons to grow up and follow in their footsteps, and my dad had become a racecar driver like his father, he didn't discuss racing with Dale when Dale was young. My brother learned about NASCAR the same way I did—by watching and listening to our dad and by being surrounded by people involved in the sport.

Dale's unusual level of exposure to NASCAR definitely gave him a desire to race, but because Dad and Teresa were both consumed with the sport, no one ever took time to identify Dale's true interests and help him pursue them.

Even though I was surrounded by cars, drivers, and pit crews more than many girls my age were, I spent most afternoons playing Barbie dolls with my neighbor. At the same time, I was also a tomboy. I loved adventure and adrenaline, and I would try almost anything. At a young age, I mastered go-karts and minibikes, always looking for a thrill. My hunger for a rush is genetic; I inherited it from my dad, and it's still a part of who I am today.

Dale, however, is not wired like I am. He loves a good adrenaline rush now, but I didn't see that side of him when we were young. He craved attention, but he didn't seek it through following rules or making good grades. While I strove to please Dad in order to *avoid* negative attention, Dale wanted Dad to take notice of him—at any cost. Unlike me, he was willing to suffer the consequences of letting Dad down, so he found ways to be noticed for all the wrong reasons. He got plenty of attention; it was just bad attention.

I realized that getting into trouble was a two-edged sword for Dale. In one way, it allowed him to gain the attention he longed for, but in other ways it was painful for him. Maybe that's why I spent so much time as a child and teenager getting him out of trouble, trying to make him feel better, looking out for him, feeling sorry for him, and helping him. For example, after meals he and I were supposed to clean our dishes, but he never did. I can't count the times I cleaned his dishes for him simply to keep him out of trouble.

At one point, the situation became so bad that Dale couldn't seem to stay out of trouble. In an effort to help him, Dad sent both of us to a Christian school. The school expelled Dale after one semester, so in 1986 Dad sent him to military school.

It's important to understand what was taking place in our family during this time. Two years earlier, Dad had started Dale Earnhardt Incorporated (DEI). NASCAR fans know that while DEI was an ownership group, my dad didn't race for them. I don't think that kind of arrangement happens in other professional sports, but it is allowable in NASCAR. Instead, he raced almost his entire career for Richard Childress Racing.

My dad and Richard Childress were extremely close friends— best friends, I would say—and hunting buddies. They were not only colleagues on the racetrack; they also traveled and spent their free time together. Richard Childress Racing's website declares, "The

Childress-Earnhardt duo was lightning in a bottle."[2] My dad was the team's only driver for twenty-five years. People have wondered why my dad continued to drive for Richard Childress even after he became an owner. Part of the answer is that he was loyal and he appreciated the opportunities and support Richard Childress had given him. All Dad ever really wanted was to own cars and to compete. His need to compete was met at Richard Childress Racing, and his desire to own cars was met through DEI.

As Dad became a sports celebrity and began earning more than enough money to live on, starting DEI made sense for him and Teresa. The company was a first-of-its-kind, personality-based business conglomerate to house all things Dale Earnhardt. He had become a sports powerhouse, and DEI was the headquarters for his personal brand as well as an entity through which he could own racecars and have his own drivers. It was not uncommon for one of his cars to race against one of Richard Childress's cars. In many ways, NASCAR is just one big family, and sometimes siblings and cousins fight!

I don't know whether the intensifying of Dale's bad behavior was related to the early years of DEI, which required so much of our dad's time and energy. I do know that I considered Dale's being sent to military school a very serious matter, and I was genuinely worried about him there. He was short and scrawny, with legs that never tanned, and I was concerned that the other students would tease him. I knew for certain that if he ever got in a fight with one of the big boys, he wouldn't win.

After three weeks of constantly worrying about Dale at military school, I decided I needed to be closer. So I asked Dad if I could go to military school too. I spent the second half of my ninth-grade year and all of my tenth-grade year there, looking after Dale. He still can't believe I wanted to go. He has often said, "Military school is like punishment. What kind of ninth grader says, 'I miss my brother. I'm going to go to military school?'"

I did.

I am not sure what compelled me to be so protective of Dale that I followed him to military school. Perhaps it was because he always chose negative ways to seek attention, and I was afraid of how bad that could become. I remember wondering at one point, *How much more trouble can you stand to get into?*

After a year and a half at military school, Dale and I both returned home to finish high school at our local public school. We fought often with Teresa and continued to take refuge in each other. Dale tried to stay out of trouble, and we both did the best we could.

I finished high school in 1990 and fulfilled one of my dad's dreams for his children—for us to go to college. Eager to move out of Dad and Teresa's house, I narrowed my college choices to three, based on discussions with our school guidance counselor and on where my friends wanted to go: Western Carolina University, Appalachian State University, and the University of North Carolina at Wilmington. Two of those schools were in the mountains, and one was near the beach. I chose the beach and enrolled at UNC Wilmington.

Since I had followed Dale to military school, he and I had both matured. He entered eleventh grade when I started my freshman year of college. Letting him go away by himself as a seventh grader when I knew other students would pick on him was one thing, but leaving him at home as a junior in high school was different. He had a driver's license by that time, so he was more independent and stable than he had ever been. I knew he would be okay, and I was eager to move away from home. For once in my life, I didn't feel bad about leaving my brother!

One of my favorite memories with my dad took place around the time of my high school graduation, not long before I left for college. The two of us went to his farm together, and on the way, we stopped at an auto parts store to buy a gas cap for a car that had been sitting in his farm shop for several weeks. To me, that white two-door Chevrolet Z24 was a genuinely cool car, unlike the SS Fastback. I would have loved to have it, but Dad was keeping it for a friend who needed to hide it before surprising his child with it.

When we arrived at the farm shop, we went to take a look at the Z24. He tossed me a gas cap, saying, "Go put this on your new car."

What? I thought. *What's he talking about?*

The car already had a gas cap. The new one was simply Dad's way of telling me the car was mine.

I never imagined that Z24 would be my graduation gift from Dad. He had never asked me what kind of car I wanted or what my dream car would be, but I was excited.

That was my high school graduation celebration. There was no special meal, no party, and no fanfare—just Dad and me in the shop with the car. It was better than any other celebration could have been.

When I left for college, I packed the Z24 and headed to Wilmington. Mom met me there to help me outfit my dorm room. I had chosen a few items before I left home but was not able to buy much, so I was thankful that Mom took me shopping for a few more essentials. Not long after I arrived, I secured a job in a retail store in the local mall in order to make spending money.

I had no idea what the future would hold. Some of what lay before me I could have never predicted, and I would change it if I could. No doubt being Dale Earnhardt's daughter has afforded me some unique *professional* advantages and opportunities, for which I will always be grateful. But my starting position didn't set me up for *personal* success. What I've learned though through the years is that you don't need to start on the pole. With enough determination and the right help, you can come from behind to win.

THREE

MOVING ON

I started my college career as a criminal justice major for no particular reason except that the subject seemed interesting. I was intrigued by the idea of following clues, investigating mysteries, and arriving at a conclusion so justice could be served. But after six months I changed my major to business, because criminal justice felt limiting. I wasn't exactly sure what I wanted to do when I finished school, but I knew a business degree would prepare me to pursue a wider variety of opportunities. I've been asked if I chose business in order to prepare myself for what I am doing today, and the answer is absolutely not! As a college student, I never dreamed that almost thirty years later I would be a racing executive.

A career related to NASCAR never entered my mind when I was younger because, although the Earnhardts are a racing family through and through, my dad and Teresa never wanted Dale or me involved in anything pertaining to the business side of racing. They worked so hard to keep us away from their business activities that I never realized working in NASCAR was an option for me. Dad never asked me what I thought I might want to do after college. He simply wanted me to have a college degree, and I suppose he assumed I would figure out how to put it to good use.

The only time I was even remotely involved with my dad's companies was one summer when I was a teenager. I worked as a receptionist at my dad's car dealership, but I only saw him once or twice when he dropped by for meetings. That was the extent of my exposure to his work life.

Whether my dad had personal reasons for not wanting me involved in the business aspects of NASCAR, I'll never know. What I do know is that Teresa seemed adamant that Dale and I not see too much or get too close to anything having to do with his interests. It seemed to us that she wanted to keep a tight grip on everything pertaining to him, and we felt she did not want us around.

Because I didn't feel there was a place for me in the Earnhardt empire, I looked toward my future with the same open-mindedness my fellow college students had—wondering what career path I might choose and assuming all options were on the table.

I missed my brother, of course, but we maintained a good relationship while I was away at school. He was Late Model racing in Myrtle Beach, South Carolina, on weekends, and when he wanted to find a sponsor for his car, I wrote the proposal for him. I occasionally made the one-and-a-half-hour trip from Wilmington to watch him race. I didn't go home often, and Dale knew why. He didn't like our family circumstances there any more than I did, so when we wanted to see each other when he wasn't racing, he traveled to Wilmington to visit me.

In addition to attending classes and enjoying an active social and sorority life, I worked a retail job at a local mall. I did well in school, mostly because I have a photographic memory, but also because I had a natural ability to understand business principles.

I was glad to have a chance to make Dad proud of me by pursuing a college degree, and maybe somewhere deep in my heart I hoped that might improve my relationship with him.

It didn't.

I continued to focus on school and work while he continued to be consumed by racing. During his rare free time, he enjoyed working on a plot of land he owned. When I called him, he typically answered the phone with a gruff "What do you need?" or "What do you want?" For some reason, I could never bring myself to say the words, "I just need your time and attention, your interest in what I'm doing."

I can't remember ever having an emotionally satisfying phone call with him, and I don't recall that he ever expressed much interest in my life or my future. During my time in Wilmington, most of our relationship took place via short phone conversations. I felt the way I had always felt—that I was still competing with the NASCAR world for my dad's attention.

Looking back now, I wonder how much of the way he related to me came from inside of him and how much reflected the way Teresa wanted him to treat me. I'll never know.

With our detached relationship you can imagine the shock I felt when on Valentine's Day during my junior year I received a beautiful bouquet of flowers from my dad. I could hardly believe my eyes when I read the message: "It's been so long since I've seen you, I've almost forgotten what you look like." That bunch of flowers and the sentiment that came with them were rare gestures from him. They made me wonder if he cared more about me than I realized, and they opened a conversation between us. We talked about the possibility of my moving back to Charlotte, getting an apartment, and finishing school there; maybe I would start racing myself, though there were barely any female drivers at the time. We agreed to make those things happen.

Three months later, during the summer of 1993, I moved back to Charlotte and enrolled at the University of North Carolina campus there. My first job in the racing industry was at a marketing company called Champion Sports Group, and I worked as many hours as my class schedule allowed. My responsibilities included answering phones, putting together press kits, and doing general administrative work. I was determined to do them all well. My desire and drive to excel may have been based in part on wanting to represent my family well, but on a deeper level it was about having someone say to me, "Good job!"

I also started Street Stock racing that summer. Dale and Kerry had bought a banged-up car that was scratched and dented everywhere except the roof. They built a roll cage inside it and rebuilt its V8 engine. I drove that at Concord Speedway, a local asphalt track, before moving on to race Late Model cars in 1994 in North Carolina, South Carolina, Tennessee, and Virginia. I raced that full-steel-body racecar with a V8 motor and 350 horsepower through the end of 1996. Our company, JRM, still races Late Model stock cars today.

By the time I graduated in December 1995, I understood how deeply ingrained racing was in me and began to think about building a career in the industry. It seemed the natural thing to do. I was happy to have college days behind me so I could focus on becoming a better driver and on finding a full-time job that would utilize my business background.

No doubt I had a huge advantage in my new job search. When your last name is Earnhardt and you're looking for a job in Charlotte, you're pretty sure doors will open easily—though I have tried very hard to never take for granted these professional advantages.

Earlier that year, Dad had added a piece to his business conglomerate when he bought a licensing company called Sports Image, which sold T-shirts, hats, die-cast race cars, and other racing memorabilia. My dad hadn't owned the rights to his name, his image, or his likeness—he had licensed them to other companies. But at the end of 1994, he began gathering all of his intellectual property to put it under his own organization. Purchasing Sports Image in 1995 allowed him to do that. That acquisition seemed to make sense; he was the center of the NASCAR universe, and products that represented him or bore his name outsold the products of other drivers tenfold.

TIME TO GO TO WORK

Once Dad acquired Sports Image, he wanted a family member to work there. I seemed to be the natural choice. I had gained some experience at Champion Sports Group, but I was only twenty-three years old and was not sure I was ready to step into a bigger role. I did it anyway. My boss, whom Dad had also hired that year, was a man named Joe Mattes, the brother-in-law of my dad's business manager.

Dad hired Joe to change the way business was done on the merchandising side of NASCAR—to take his merchandising from a cottage industry to a well-run, profitable, professional company.

Joe had worked at the company only four weeks when I interviewed with him, though he had long considered my dad his mentor in the business aspects of NASCAR. I didn't know for many years that my dad told Joe when he hired him at Sports Image, "I will never tell you who to hire. You make those decisions yourself."

On the early February day in 1995 when I went to my job interview with Joe, my dad hadn't told him that his appointment was with me. I have no recollection of that day, but Joe says when I first saw him that afternoon, he said hello and he was glad to see me. Then, having no idea why I was in the building, he asked, "What are you doing here?"

I simply responded, "I'm here for an interview with you."

"What's the deal?" Joe asked, still surprised and definitely curious. I don't remember much about my answer, but he does:

Kelley said, "I've just graduated college, and I'm looking for a job. I'm just wondering if you think I would fit in around here and if there are ways you think I could help."

Being the daughter of Dale Earnhardt meant expectations for Kelley were high. She couldn't avoid that. The same was true for Dale Jr. As she went on to express a desire to get to know our fans, to learn more about how race team sponsorships work, and to understand our business model, I could tell that this fiery, energetic, passionate young woman was also very smart. What she said to me punched all the right buttons. I could see that she did not need to learn what racing's two key components are—the power of the fan base and the value of sponsorships. Racing is a fan sport, and because of the fans, good things happen. It's also a sponsorship sport, and without the sponsors, nobody goes anywhere. As a third-generation racer, she must have watched and listened a lot, because the business of NASCAR was innate and organic in her.[1]

In 1997, Dad sold Sports Image and Joe Mattes left the company. I understood why Dad sold the business: the buyer, a die-cast manufacturer, made him a financial offer too lucrative to decline. The new owners, a company called Action Performance, considered me an asset and liked having me on their team. I enjoyed the work and was doing well, so I never thought about leaving. Sports Image and Action Performance merged under the name Action Performance, and the new owner took the company public. I worked there until 2001, learning the ins and outs of the merchandising side of NASCAR and gaining experience that would prove vital to me later.

My time at Sports Image / Action Performance proved to be almost as helpful as my time in college earning a business degree. By the end of my first year I had become the lead account person for Food City and Snap-On Tools, two sponsors of my dad's cars, and for Mom and Pop's Western Steer restaurants, who sponsored my Late Model car with my brothers. As sponsors, they were important players in the NASCAR world.

I learned so many important lessons during my time there, but one practice that seemed to develop naturally—and quickly became one of the best business practices I learned—was to ask the accounts, "How can we support you and help you reach your goals?" I didn't ask the question because I read in a business book that expressing that kind of interest would endear me to my clients. In fact, I never read *anything* about what questions to ask. I inquired because I really cared. I was developing relationships with people in those organizations, and I realized that we were all part of the NASCAR family together. I genuinely wanted them to succeed. I know that might seem unnecessary, but it was part of who I was in those early days of my career, and it's still a part of who I am today.

FOUR

THEN EVERYTHING CHANGED

Sunday, February 18, 2001, started out just like many other NASCAR race days for me. I was a twenty-seven-year-old single mother to a beautiful five-month-old baby girl named Karsyn. She and I were at Mamaw Earnhardt's house to watch my dad and Dale compete in the race at Daytona International Speedway.

On the last lap, Dale and his teammate, Michael Waltrip, were in front of my dad, leading the race, when Dad's car crashed into the wall. It was a sight we had seen before, so we weren't overly concerned. We simply waited, watching for Dad to climb out of the car like he always did.

Time slowed to a crawl as we continued to stare at the television screen. We saw no sign of Dad—just a mangled number 3 car surrounded by the safety crew that was trying to extricate him. Within minutes, we knew in our hearts that this was no common racecar accident. It was serious.

Then the phone rang. My dad's brother, Uncle Danny, who was at the race as a member of Dale's racing team, gave my grandmother and me the news that my forty-nine-year-old dad had been killed in the crash.

We both shrieked in horror, then burst into tears and sobbed as we held each other. I quickly called Karsyn's paternal grandparents and asked them to pick her up so I could focus my full attention on the horrendous tragedy that had just rocked us.

A crowd of family and friends soon filled my grandmother's house. At some point, I spoke briefly with Dale by phone. Dale, Uncle Danny, and the rest of the team flew back to Charlotte as quickly as possible on the DEI plane and joined us at my grandmother's. Television news stories about the crash filled the airwaves almost as soon as it happened, and around ten o'clock that night, news crews showed up outside her home in the next phase of what became a huge media event as shock and sadness reached around the world.

My memories of the week following my dad's death are still blurry. Teresa didn't want Dale, Kerry, or me to see his body at the funeral home, claiming that she wanted to preserve our memories of him as we knew him, not in a casket.

We held a private family service on Wednesday at our family church. On Thursday, we held a public service at a very large church in Charlotte, which holds about six thousand people. We also attended a brief employee gathering at DEI, where everyone was in shock at the loss. On Friday, Dale had to travel to Rockingham for the next race.

Sometimes people I've never met recognize me and say, "I sure do miss your dad." Occasionally, they say it with such feeling that I can tell his death actually affected them emotionally. They talk about him the way other people talk about losing a beloved spouse or family member. To them, he was a favorite celebrity racecar driver, but to me, he was Dad. In their own way, these people do miss him, but his death did not leave them the memories, the longing, the love, the unanswered questions, and the unfulfilled hope it left in me. All those thoughts go through my mind when people tell me they miss him, but typically all I say is, "Yeah. I miss him too." They couldn't possibly know how emotionally loaded that statement is for me.

THE STORY THAT'S NEVER BEEN TOLD

People have no idea how much I miss my dad and how deeply I wish the two of us could have developed a closer relationship as we grew older. During the year or so before he passed away, I had the faintest glimmer of hope that the relationship between us might improve.

When I became pregnant in January 2000, I was worried about how my dad would react. My boyfriend worked on one of his race teams and, like many other people, viewed my dad as intimidating. He was literally sweating when the two of us broke the news to him. My dad took it surprisingly well and began to offer some fatherly advice. "Don't be in a hurry to get married," he told us. "Don't make any crazy decisions."

My dad didn't know that I didn't want to marry my baby's father. In fact, we had been fighting for weeks. Soon, we stopped seeing each other completely. Before Karsyn was born, I began seeing someone else I had dated previously. My dad was very angry with me because he didn't approve of the situation, and my relationship with him shut down altogether.

He did visit me in the hospital after Karsyn was born in

September 2000, and he fell in love with her instantly. When she was about a month old, she and I attended a Halloween party at DEI. He carried her around, smiling and showing her off to everyone there. I wondered—and hoped—as I watched him dote on her, *Is this the beginning of a whole new relationship for us? Will his love for my daughter open his heart to the love that* his *daughter has longed for all her life?* I desperately wanted the answer to be yes. Maybe in time it would have been. But he was killed only three and a half months later.

Even though he was enamored with Karsyn, Dad and I had a strained relationship. After she came into our lives, we spoke more than we had spoken over the preceding months, but to say that we were truly on speaking terms wouldn't be accurate. When he died, we hadn't talked with each other in three weeks.

Part of what made my dad's passing even more heartbreaking and traumatic was that it happened during the most difficult season of our father-daughter journey. I will always believe that just before that fateful Daytona race, we had reached the point where we wanted to rectify things between us, but time did not allow for that. The words of reconciliation that I longed to speak—and perhaps he did too—would remain forever silent.

I carried the weight and guilt of that for years.

WHAT DO WE DO NOW?

As everyone affected by Dad's death struggled to find a new normal, Dale and I found ourselves uncertain about many aspects of our lives. But one thing we knew for sure was that Teresa would take charge of everything pertaining to my dad's racing career, business interests, and personal affairs.

We also knew that Teresa would be in charge of Dale's career, because at that time he was driving for DEI and enjoying unprecedented success on the racetrack. Because of Dale's accomplishments, Dad had established JR Motorsports for him in 1999. It was simply a business entity, almost a façade. It was nothing more than an official address for Dale to receive payments for winnings, a tiny company in which one person answered fan mail, sent autographs on request, and paid bills. It also served as a legal name to put on his contracts.

DEI managed other aspects of Dale's career, such as public relations, personal service endorsements, and various agreements. They handled his business without consulting him very much and made decisions on his behalf in their best interest, not his. However, as long as our dad was alive, he made sure Dale was not taken advantage of. Maybe everything was not as advantageous as it could have been for Dale, but Dad certainly ensured that he didn't suffer.

Dale and I never thought working with Teresa would be easy because of our history of conflict and tension with her. Though he and I both hoped he could continue racing for DEI, we felt certain that his driving for Teresa's organization would have its challenges. As Dale tried to work with DEI during the months following Dad's death, I saw him struggling. For various reasons, he simply wasn't getting the support he needed as a driver.

It was as if DEI went on autopilot after Dad's accident. Teresa immediately turned her attention to fighting an intense legal battle over the release of the autopsy photos, and the managers at DEI were just keeping the company going. As I watched from a distance,

I became increasingly convinced that the company wasn't looking out for Dale and his interests—as my dad would have wanted—and I was losing hope that they would ever do so. Plus, in a matter of a few years, Dale had gone from making a few hundred dollars per week to making millions, which called for an entirely new level of management and business expertise.

Because I had no part in DEI, I was powerless to help Dale. I still worked at Action Performance and had become vice president of procurement, overseeing the purchase of all products from our vendors and suppliers. Though I was happy with my job and salary—at just twenty-eight years old I was already making six figures—I needed to leave. Action Performance understandably wanted to capitalize on merchandise and memorabilia related to my dad, but DEI wouldn't allow it. The longer DEI delayed, the more awkward the situation became for me.

At the same time, I was growing increasingly concerned about Dale's business relationship with DEI. All my life I had looked out for my brother. When he started racing, his relationship with Dad improved, and Dad made sure the business aspect of Dale's career was handled properly. I trusted Dad in that regard and was happy to see him involved in Dale's life that way. Once Dad was gone, I was certainly willing for someone else to manage Dale's business, but in the context of DEI, he wasn't surrounded by people we felt we could trust to do it well. He needed more than just a person to see that his contracts were signed and his winnings were properly accounted for. He needed an advocate, someone who was on his side, someone who really knew and understood him and who would look out for his best interests. I knew my brother would need me not only as the big sister and friend I had always been to him but as someone who could provide management and financial experience, which I had been gaining at Sports Image and Action Performance since 1995.

By August 2001, I knew what I had to do. I called Dale and simply said, "Dad's gone, and no one at DEI is looking out for your best interests. This is not going to be good for you. You're at a point where you really need someone to manage your finances and your business, someone to help you with everything that's going on in your career."

Dale knew exactly what I meant without my having to say it more plainly: I wanted to work with him, even though I was thriving in my current job and had worked hard to be in the position I held. He also knew it paid much better than he could pay me, so his immediate response was, "I can't afford you." He didn't understand the scope of work I knew I needed to do for him. He felt I was worth more—and doing more—in my current role than he envisioned I could do for him.

I knew he would say that, so I had my answer ready: "I'll take a 50 percent pay cut." That's how strongly I felt I needed to be involved with his business.

On August 26, 2001, I officially went to work for Dale. My goals when I started the job were clear: I wanted to look out for my brother in a whole new way, and I wanted to make business decisions that would benefit him. I knew my dad had always done that, and I thought I would do a better job than Teresa would. Dale doesn't like conflict, so I also felt that to a certain extent he might be tempted to let people walk all over him. I didn't want anyone taking advantage of Dale. I knew how to keep that from happening, and I was determined to do so.

My strategy was simple: I would begin to separate his business interests from DEI. I did that slowly and deliberately. First, I made sure I had a seat at the table anytime any discussion pertaining to Dale took place. For the seven months between our dad's death and my joining JRM, not everyone involved in meetings or decisions that affected Dale prioritized him. I changed that immediately when I joined his team. Second, I worked to gain oversight of his assets. Pursing these two objectives required patience and diligence, because creating distance between Dale's business interests and DEI was not well received at DEI. At the time, I didn't intend for Dale and me to start our own company. He and I both simply wanted to see him less entangled with the organization.

In 2004, we won a big victory when Teresa agreed to release Dale's naming rights and trademarks to JRM, which still operated under the DEI umbrella. Dale and I both viewed this as a significant positive development, and we thought it would be possible for Dale's business interests to remain part of DEI. So I negotiated a new three-year contract between Dale and DEI, under which he would continue to drive for them until 2007.

But as the end of the contract drew near, the need to secure a new agreement for Dale weighed heavily on my mind. Throughout the latter half of 2006, I tried to negotiate a deal for him to continue to drive for DEI. I worked hard on it but found the process difficult and frustrating. Lack of communication, inadequate responses, missed meetings, and a refusal to compromise on matters that were important to Dale and me eventually caused me to realize a new agreement would not be possible.

At that point, Dale and I took a big step forward and offered to purchase DEI. The leadership there set the selling price so ridiculously high that we couldn't possibly have afforded it—and as a businesswoman, I wasn't willing to buy an overvalued company. Dale and I finally saw the truth: Teresa had no desire for the two of us to remain part of our dad's organization.

As Dale once said, our relationship with Teresa "ain't a bed of roses."[1] The animosity, resentment, and conflict that had characterized our relationship for years became so intense that we knew we could no longer work with DEI. From that moment, our priority became taking care of Dale, not staying with our late father's business simply because of our last name. We were satisfied that we had done everything we could possibly do to stay, but the time had come for us to leave Dale Earnhardt Incorporated. It was drastic and risky, but in May 2007, we announced the decision.

By the time the 2008 racing season started, Dale had made big news in the NASCAR world by joining Hendrick Motorsports, owned by racing legend Rick Hendrick. This move seemed shocking on multiple levels: people without knowledge of our situation couldn't believe we would leave our dad's company, and people who were aware of it expected Dale to drive for Richard Childress Racing, where Dad had driven for so long.

If I had to summarize the three reasons we joined Hendrick, they would be *relationship*, *trust*, and *flexibility*. Rick Hendrick has been a family friend for many years, and Dale and I have known him all of our lives. He and my maternal grandfather, Robert Gee, an excellent racecar builder, were close friends and colleagues as far back as their days as young men in Virginia. In 1983, they even owned a winning racecar together, with my dad behind the wheel. In addition, my brother Dale was good friends with Mr. Hendrick's son, Ricky.

When Grandfather Gee suffered a stroke and was unable to

work, Mr. Hendrick remained a loyal friend to him. I was very involved in my grandfather's care, so every time Mr. Hendrick visited him in the hospital or at home, I got to know him better. I was aware of Mr. Hendrick's excellent reputation as a racing professional, but after my grandfather's stroke, I quickly gained a sense of love and respect for him as a person, and I recognized him as someone Dale and I could trust. Before long, he became more than a friend to us. To this day, we think of him as family.

NASCAR fans know that one of the great tragedies in our sport took place in October 2004, when a Hendrick Motorsports plane carrying ten people crashed on the way to a race in Virginia. That day, Mr. Hendrick lost his son, his brother, two nieces, and some of the best people he had ever worked with. Dale and I had suffered our own NASCAR tragedy when our dad died, so we grieved for Mr. Hendrick in an intensely personal way.

Mr. Hendrick was one of the first people we spoke with when we started looking for a new home for Dale's racing career, armed with a multipage document detailing what we needed in a new ownership relationship. We were open to other options and met with other owners, but we knew from the beginning that Mr. Hendrick would probably be a good place for Dale to land. Relationally, our trust in Mr. Hendrick was solid. Competitively, we believed Mr. Hendrick could deliver. But before we made the business arrangement official, we needed one final detail to fall into place—and we were asking for something unusual. To my knowledge, it was unprecedented in our sport.

I wanted to keep JRM as its own business entity that would maintain control of some key functions of Dale's career—marketing and public relations, brand management and development, and other matters, which normally would have been controlled by the team. Although my desires didn't reflect standard operating procedure in NASCAR, Mr. Hendrick was willing to negotiate each point to my satisfaction. I had been looking for that kind of flexibility and was thrilled to find it with a man we so respected and loved.

At the time, Hendrick Motorsports had only one Xfinity team (the second tier of NASCAR racing, similar to minor leagues in other sports), just like we did at JRM. We were surprised—but thrilled—that they were willing to merge that team with JRM. In 2008 Mr. Hendrick became a part owner with Dale of JRM, and I joined them in ownership in 2010.

While our relationship with Mr. Hendrick is professionally beneficial, it's also personally redemptive for us both. The fact that we lost our dad and he lost his son has bonded us in a unique way. We will always honor the memories of our loved ones and wish we had had more time with them, but for Dale and me—and hopefully for Mr. Hendrick too—the pain, emptiness, and bitterness of our losses have been made sweeter because of the life and the love that we now share together.

PART TWO

LESSONS LEARNED

My goal in part 2 of this book is to share with you the lessons I've learned growing up as the daughter of Dale Earnhardt Sr. and in my current role as vice president and co-owner of JR Motorsports. Now that you have heard some of my story, I think you'll understand more about how I came to value these lessons and why I think they're so important.

Some lessons I learned watching racecars vie for position on the track or listening to conversations among pit crews. Some I learned through the therapy that helped me make peace with my past and become willing to embrace a better future. Other lessons I learned sitting at my desk, reviewing contracts, managing financials to make sense in a competitive sport with large amounts of money at stake, or trying to figure out how to best manage people, our most valuable resource. I am grateful for them all, and I hope they serve you well.

FIVE

BE AUTHENTIC AND APPROACHABLE

In Xfinity Series races, where we compete, races are held on Fridays and Saturdays, thirty-three weekends a year. We have forty racecars, and we send eight of them to the race location each weekend of the season—one primary car and one backup car for each of our four teams. A total of forty cars compete in each race, and the maximum number of cars any owner can enter is four. As of 2019, JRM is the only owner with four teams competing.

After each race, cars return to our shop in Mooresville, North Carolina, via tractor-trailer trucks. When the checkered flag falls in one race, we immediately turn our focus to the next green flag, usually six days later. First thing Monday morning after a race weekend, our team begins tearing down the cars used the previous weekend and rebuilding them for the next weekend's races. Their work is not like building passenger cars, which are mass-produced with standard equipment. Each of our racecars is a unique piece of specialized machinery designed to get the driver across the finish line safely and faster than anyone else.

In addition to my responsibilities at JRM, where I'm a business owner and a boss, I'm also a wife and a mother. Many days my husband, L.W., who is a valuable member of our JRM team, drops by my office to discuss various work issues or just to go to lunch with me. Sometimes my children do their homework in my office or play on their phones while I finish my work in the afternoons. Our family also has a dog we love very much, and it's not unusual for him to be lounging under my worktable in the office.

I take my job and my responsibilities seriously, but I don't pretend to be 100 percent boss 100 percent of the time. I'm determined not to act as though I don't have a husband or a family when I am at work. For me, part of being real is saying "This is who I am. Every member of my family is important to me, just as this organization is important to me. If I'm going to lead this company, my family will be in and out of the office at times. In addition, I'll also be in and out at times, because my children have only one first day of kindergarten. They have only one high school graduation. They'll have many milestones that matter to them and to me, and I'm going to be there for all of them. I may be working at midnight to compensate for time out of the office, but I *will* get my job done. I'm determined to lead this organization effectively while also fulfilling my responsibilities at home."

Sometimes I have to get creative in order to do everything I need to do. I prioritize some activities over others because there are only so many hours in each day. That's part of being a real leader with a real life.

I know what it feels like to pretend to be someone I'm not. I refuse to do that anymore. If you are ever tempted to do it, I hope you'll refuse too. Trying to fake anything leads only to conflict and unhappiness. In contrast, learning to be authentic has been not only personally rewarding but also integral to my business life.

REAL LEADERS ARE THE BEST LEADERS

Being authentic and approachable is another way of saying, "Be real." In fact, I would feel I was losing in every way if I couldn't be authentic with the people around me. Being real is something I require of myself, and it takes many forms. It may mean being brutally honest while still being kind. It may mean asking for help when I need it. Or it may mean making a decision that I know in my heart is right, though my head cannot tell me exactly why.

I believe real leaders are the best leaders. Many people have a sixth sense about the people in leadership roles in their lives. Whether that person is a CEO, a schoolteacher, a pastor, a board chair, or the leader of a neighborhood garage sale, we are sensitive to phony people. We *know* when someone is not authentic, and we don't like it. People who try to fake it may seem to thrive for a while, but they rarely achieve true or lasting success.

I grew up in the shadow of a famous racecar driver, a bigger-than-life personality around whom I felt I *couldn't* be real. In order to remain in my dad's good graces, I felt that I had to be who he and the people around him wanted me to be—not who I truly was. I did not want to disappoint him. Maybe that's why I try so hard to teach my children not to be someone they're not or not to pretend to be a certain type of person simply to impress or win favor with someone else. I speak to them about this every day, but that's not nearly as powerful as living it in front of them.

I didn't enjoy sharing my dad with thousands of fans, but I couldn't stick my tongue out at them or tell them to go away—even if I really wanted to. Sometimes I felt that way because I believed they were taking my dad away from me. But I lived by the unwritten rule that I had to behave certain ways because fans were watching.

To be clear, the fact that my dad wasn't available to me was not about the fans; my dad's passion for racing simply didn't leave much room for anything else in his life. As a child, all I knew was that everywhere I went, I was part of a family that seemed to exist to serve a legion of others—people I had not met and did not know. In my mind, they dictated too much about my life, and I couldn't understand why making them happy was so important. It took a few years for me to understand how much they mean to our sport and to realize that they were not taking my dad away from me; they were simply excited to see him.

Now that I'm older, I genuinely love, appreciate, and value our fans. I'm convinced NASCAR fans are the best fans in the world. We wouldn't exist without them, and on some level, everything I do in my roles as a NASCAR executive and member of the Earnhardt family ultimately influences the fan experience. I want that experience to be amazing for them. Helping them enjoy everything NASCAR offers brings me joy and satisfaction.

BEING REAL MEANS BEING HONEST

I know now that my job is to be true to myself, not to make anyone else happy. Ten years ago, I couldn't have brought myself to share the truths I have about my father because I would've been afraid that something I said about my dad would somehow reflect badly on my brother. When Dale and I were younger, trying to paint a perfect picture of our family didn't seem to matter as much to him as it did to me. He never hesitated to dye his hair, and his reputation for partying is well known. The fans never seemed to judge him negatively for that; it was all part of his persona. As I saw the situation, he was free to do whatever he wanted to do to affect his public image, but I didn't want to risk damaging it.

I'll never know whether candidly sharing my struggles with my father would've had negative consequences for Dale. What I do know is that I still have great love in my heart for my dad. Honoring his memory as best I can is important to me, but I'm no longer willing to protect a false image. I need to be real about who he was because that helps me be real about who I am.

If you have someone in your life with whom you have a complicated relationship, I hope you will be real about that person too. Understand that people who see you from a distance don't know the full story. They're only aware of what a person does in public and of the image that person has created. They base their judgments only on what they do know, even if it is incomplete or incorrect.

It's so important to be real, but being real is risky. That kind of vulnerability puts a person at risk for rejection and disappointment and for being misunderstood and judged. Having tried to live as someone I wasn't—and having now learned to be who I truly am—I can say that while the risks are real, they're also worth taking. You will gain more than you lose. You will find a sense of inner peace that can't be explained, and you will enjoy the satisfaction and rewards of living an authentic life.

ALLOW OTHERS TO BE REAL TOO

Part of being authentic in a business environment means making an effort to help others feel they can be real too. That includes respecting and listening to someone who presents fresh ideas or takes different paths to a goal, whether that person is a new entry-level hire or someone who has worked in the business for decades. I've learned to be willing to rethink a situation, to recalibrate our route to success if the ideas are good and workable, or even to disrupt our old way of doing things in favor of a new and better way.

In some work environments, innovation is encouraged—in theory. It may even be included in the company's values. But when employees actually introduce a new idea, management feels threatened and downplays the attempt at creativity or presents it to superiors without giving the employee credit for it. Employees then feel silenced and disrespected.

I would like to think that JRM is a place that appreciates and makes space for innovation, as long as it's done respectfully. We can't upset our workflow with unproductive or poorly conceived ideas, and we can't allow negative employees to affect the entire company. But if someone tries to break a mold with a good heart and in an attitude of humility, I want to respect that person. That one employee who dares to be different may lead our organization to a completely new and wonderful way of doing business.

MAKE YOURSELF APPROACHABLE

Another way to be real is to be accessible to the people who keep your company going. Maintaining an attitude of professionalism in your role is important, but being in charge doesn't have to mean acting bossy or aloof. You can be friendly, genuinely interested in the people around you, and easily approachable and accessible.

I've heard that people have said of me, "She can see all sides of an issue. She's a great analytical thinker. She knows how to solve problems. She understands the consequences and potential results of different decisions. She clearly sees and articulates pros and cons." I appreciate all of these descriptions, but I think what I most like to hear is "She's approachable" or "She's accessible."

Being approachable is more than a goal to me; it's a value. I deeply desire for people to feel they can talk to me and that they can be honest. I start by making an effort to know each employee by name. It feels good to walk into our race shop and hear the mechanics say, "Hi, Kelley!" I have to assume that when I respond with "Hi, Jake," "Hi, Carl," or "Hi, Terry," that makes them feel good too. This is an easy way to show that I notice them and care enough about them to call them by name. I do the same thing as I walk around our accounting office or down the hallways in our marketing area.

NASCAR is a small world, so I occasionally meet people who come to work for us and find out that their uncle worked for my dad or that their neighbor works in our human resources department. Making those family or friendship connections is important. As much as possible, I try to remember those details, and people appreciate that.

Another simple example of making myself accessible is this:

if I want a bottle of water while I am working, I get some money from my purse and walk to the vending machine, just as every other employee is expected to do. My assistant would be happy to do that for me, but I do it personally—not just because I think it's the right thing to do, but because it is a way to be accessible to the people I lead. I don't hold impromptu meetings while getting water, but I do use those opportunities to smile and greet employees, ask them how they're doing, and say, "Have a great afternoon!" This is one of many quick and easy ways to connect with people. It allows me access to them, and hopefully that causes them to realize I am accessible too.

In late 2018, a new JRM driver named Noah Gragson visited our facility and brought some family members and friends with him. He was standing in our shop, surrounded by his guests, when I walked in with my arms full of boxes that needed to go in the trash. When I saw the group, I simply said, "Hi! You guys caught me on my way to the dumpster." They seemed surprised, and they, along with others in the shop, offered to take the boxes for me.

I appreciated the offers, but I don't ever want anyone to think I expect people to do things for me when I can do them myself. People all over our company take their own boxes to the dumpster, and I can do that too. I'm not above doing it, and I do not want anyone to think that I am.

Not long after that incident, L.W. and I were on my way to pick up Rick Hendrick for our company Christmas party. My car was not as clean as I wanted it to be, so I pulled it around to our shop and asked, "Do we have a shop vac handy?"

L.W. wanted me to let one of the workers, who had offered, vacuum for me, but there was no reason I couldn't do it myself. Plus, I don't feel comfortable letting other people clean out my personal car or clean up my personal mess. I try to keep everything real. L.W. understands that, and his encouragement to let someone else vacuum the car wasn't about my not being real; it was about the fact that he thinks I deserve better—and I love him for that!

Across our company, people volunteer to do personal tasks for me, but I hardly ever take them up on their offers because I want to keep us all on a level playing field. I need to maintain their respect for my knowledge, my leadership, and my position, but I don't ever want to take advantage of it.

"Because management says so" and "because we've always done it that way" are two common leadership responses that shut people down quickly and send the message that a leader is not approachable. When people have legitimate questions about why we do certain things, those responses are not helpful. They're old-fashioned answers that reflect an outdated mind-set toward leadership and collaboration. Sometimes "the way we have always done things" needs to change, and sometimes managers need to stop and think about what they are asking of people instead of expecting their word to become company law. As leaders, we don't need to feel pressured to justify our decisions, but we are wise to want the people around us to understand our thinking so they can support and participate in our corporate vision and efforts.

At JRM and in companies around the world, I would love to see the phrases "because management says so" and "because that's the way we've always done it" traded in for thoughtful, articulate explanations employees can understand and embrace. Growing up, I often felt I did not get the answers I needed to my sincere questions, and that's probably why helping people feel they can approach me and be heard and respected is so important to me now.

This holds true in my personal life too. Sometimes my children ask, "Why do you have to work all the time?" I try to answer them honestly and not just by taking the easy way out, which would be to say something like, "Because everybody works." Instead, I respond with questions that will help them understand what's going on so that they can form their own conclusions. Our conversations go something like this:

"Mom, why do you have to work so much?"

"Do you like where we live?" (They do.)

"Do you like being able to go to the grocery store with me and buy some things you want?" (Yes.)

"Do you like to play extracurricular sports and do things with your friends?" (They like that too.)

"Do you like to go on vacation?" (They *really* like that.)

As they answer my questions, they realize why I work so much: so we can live the life we enjoy. But I'm also quick to let them know that because of the racing season schedule, I do have to work some weekends, but I can take more time off during the summers than most parents can.

Real leadership in a business setting doesn't consist of sending emails and barking orders. It's more interactive than that: it's saying what we need to say, when we need to say it, and standing firm in our positions while also being authentic, accessible, and open-minded.

Being real is a bold action. It requires the courage to break the images and expectations others may have of us and to live and lead from the very core of our beings. Anyone who operates with that level of authenticity is someone who inspires good work, loyalty, and a willingness to make great things happen.

SIX

KNOW HOW TO MAKE DECISIONS

One morning I woke up early and found L.W. intently studying his iPad. When I asked what he was up to, he explained that he was reading about various fences, fencing materials, and different kinds of trees—how durable or hardy some are, how nicely some of the fencing materials age in the weather, how quickly some kinds of trees grow, what they cost, and the maintenance comparisons. Let's just say it was much more than I wanted to know so early in the morning.

L.W. had visions of our property being a nature preserve for wild animals, such as deer and turkey. He wanted them to be able to roam freely and did not like the fence that surrounded our property, so he was trying to decide whether to put up a new a fence or to line our driveway with maturing trees.

Normally, I'm the one who wants to know all the details about a decision before I make it. But where the fence was concerned, I thought the best course of action was simply to talk to the people at a local farm store, make a decision, and order what they recommended. We both care about our home and property, but I wasn't ready to do such extensive research. On the other hand, L.W. wanted to be armed with knowledge before he arrived at the store.

"We know we don't like the fence we currently have," I told him. "So let's just do *something* by getting rid of that one. Then we can think about what to do next."

To me, the first decision was clear. Before we could do anything else, we needed to tear down the old fence. In L.W.'s mind, however, the better course of action was to leave up the old fence until we had a solid plan for what to do next—what the new fence would look like and be made of and how we would incorporate trees. He thought that we should at least have some type of fence until the new one was ready to be installed. At the end of the conversation we realized that it was just a fence. We would make the best decision we could, and if we didn't like it, we could change it.

Within a few months, the old fence came down, and we decided not to replace it. Instead, we planted trees in certain carefully planned places. We love how they look, and we've seen an increase in deer going through that area of our pasture. Without a fence, the house and yard look much more open and expansive, which we also love. L.W. did his due diligence on this project, and we couldn't be happier with the results.

Our lives are filled with the need to make decisions. And unlike our situation with the fence, many of those decisions directly impact other people's lives and livelihoods.

Good decision-making is one of the strengths I've had to work hard to develop. For some decisions I know I need to take my time and do the research. But others need to be made quickly, which is vitally important in a fast-paced business such as racing. And

I'm not intimidated by the fact that I might not always get it right. There comes a point in every situation, as with the fence for our house, where it's best to choose *something* because it's the only way to move forward.

I asked Joe Mattes what he thinks about how I have changed as a decision-maker over the years. He said:

> When I think about your early years versus now, I would say that in the early years you mainly wanted to get across the finish line. You wanted to fix the problems or answer the questions—whatever the problems and questions were. You were eager to put a matter behind you and move forward. What you learned in those early years was how to assess information quickly, how to get your hands on important facts, and who to seek answers from when you had questions. Now, you're not as emotional as you once were. You gather facts better. You take time to sleep on a situation. Your ability to live with your decisions and deal with their consequences has changed over time. But one thing has always been true: you're not afraid to make one![1]

I agree with his assessment. I could have thought about things more, asked more questions, or taken more time with certain decisions. Even though I'm wired to move on as soon as possible after making a choice, I've learned to be willing to review anything I might see as a bad decision if I think it will move my life or my company forward. Anyone who works with me would say that if I feel a decision has not served JRM well, I'm quick to gather the people who helped make it and the ones most affected by it so we can discuss and learn from it. For me, that's part of being a responsive leader.

PRINCIPLES OF GREAT DECISION-MAKING

Every decision has a reason behind it, both in business and in life. However, I want to focus in this chapter specifically on decision-making in business. Sometimes the reason for a business decision is purely practical: You want to beat the competition. You want to stay on budget and on schedule. You want to hire the best talent in your industry. You want to invest in the future strength of your company. You want everyone on the team to be more efficient.

While there are all kinds of practical reasons for the choices you make, you can also rely on certain principles to guide you. These principles do not relate to the logistics or particulars of your circumstances; they are ideals that apply to every situation.

Principle #1: Do the Right Thing—Always

My number one consideration when making a decision is a principle my dad taught me: do the right thing. He believed in doing the right thing always, in every situation. Because of that, doing the right thing has been forged into my character for as long as I can remember. I think about it every day, in every decision I make.

The obvious and easy way to determine whether a decision is the right thing is to ask the following questions: Is it legal? Is it ethical? Is it honest? Does it have integrity? If the answer to any of those questions is no, then it's not the right thing to do. But beyond those basic qualifications for doing right, there are other considerations specific to your personal situation.

For me, doing the right thing when making decisions includes aiming to benefit the greatest number of people in the most significant ways. It also means—even in the cutthroat world of competitive sports—being kindhearted, not mean-spirited. It means making decisions that are not only good for our company but also benefit our sport as a whole. I appreciate the way Joe Mattes describes this:

> In the early days of JRM, we gave up real dollars at times in order to do the right thing. When you're 40 percent of the market, as we are, you have weight and influence in your industry. We do not use that for ourselves; we ask what is best for the industry globally. We have lost money at times because we think that way, but it's the right thing to do. Kelley and Dale Jr. have such a deep and genuine respect for the heritage of the sport, which came from their dad, that making decisions in the best interest of NASCAR is second nature for them. It's in their DNA. The decision-making process that Kelley leads at JRM always asks, "What's the right thing to do for the sport?" She and Dale are number one in that category. Undisputed.[2]

Honoring my dad's example of doing the right thing is one of the ways I keep his legacy alive. It has cost us money at times, but I would rather lose a few dollars than compromise our integrity.

A person can always defend doing the right thing. An interviewer once asked me if I run my company according to my own personal values and principles. Of course, I said yes. I can't imagine doing it any differently. I would think most people run their companies according to their own values; it's just that some people's values start and end with deceit and dishonesty. That's not how I think. I'm committed to honesty and integrity from start to finish, in every aspect of our organization and in everything I do.

To do the right thing means removing one's own motives and viewing options holistically. I once had a manager who considered only how decisions would affect her personally; whether she supported a decision depended on what it meant for her instead of how it could benefit all employees, the company's bottom line, and the services we were attempting to provide. Another employee used and abused every privilege available regarding paid time off and other perks. This employee continually manipulated situations and gave excuses for working the system. Both of these people were blinded by selfish motives, so they were unable to see the way their decisions affected others. I do my best to do the right thing, and I expect employees to do the same.

Principle #2: Timing Is Everything

There have been times when I've had the feeling of being blocked or hindered in my decision-making. I've learned to respect that feeling because, more often than not, I've realized later that I felt restrained for a good reason. I couldn't explain it at the time; it was just an instinct. Eventually I came to trust that this instinct is a valid cause for not moving forward.

If something will not let you move forward, stay still. You may not know why you do not feel free to act, but don't struggle to figure it out. Trust your gut. Chances are, you will realize later why you didn't feel free to make the decision or you'll see the wisdom of not pushing ahead when you did not feel peaceful about it.

It's important to consider *when* to act. Taking your time is fine as long as you're working through the four steps of decision-making outlined later in this chapter. Taking your time doesn't mean you're procrastinating or being indecisive; it means that you want to be deliberate and give yourself the opportunity to thoughtfully consider all the relevant factors, especially since due diligence is necessary in most major decisions.

A few years ago, L.W. and I began looking for a house. At times I became impatient and wanted to make a decision quickly. Maybe a given property didn't check all the boxes, but it checked nine out of ten. But L.W. wanted to wait, and waiting proved to be the right decision. We eventually found exactly what we were looking for, and we were ready to pounce on it when we did. The house has been just right for us, and two years later, I still say to L.W., "This is the most perfect place for our family." I'm so glad we waited. We had the time, so we made sure to check all ten boxes and eventually found the place we now call home.

Principle #3: Keep First Things First

It's important to determine the urgency and importance of your decisions. Some become priorities because of time or schedule, while others are priorities because of their value to you or your organization. Time-driven decisions often need to be made quickly in order to keep productivity or momentum from grinding to a halt or to avoid missing out on a particular opportunity. In contrast, values-driven decisions are rarely urgent. Be honest with yourself; if you're not ready to make that kind of decision, you will not fail to gain because you waited. It's okay to say, "This is important, so I'm not going to make a decision about it until I truly believe I'm ready."

FOUR STEPS TO QUALITY DECISIONS

Once you understand the principles of good decision-making, you'll be ready to put them into practice. I've distilled what I've learned about how to do this into four steps. These are as applicable to your personal life as they are to your life on the job.

Step #1: Begin at the End

One of the first things I consider when trying to make a quality decision is not the decision itself but my ultimate goal. I look at the big picture and ask myself, *What is the end result I want to see here?* Then, I make decisions that will move me toward that desired end.

We should always be thinking ahead. If we can view the decisions before us—both the big ones and the small ones—in the context of our long-term strategies instead of seeing them simply as independent choices, we can use them as stepping-stones to reach our goals.

Step #2: Get the Facts

When making a decision, I seek out all the data I can get, along with the pros and cons of every possible option. I want to understand why we might want to go in a certain direction—and why not. In addition, I find out who will be involved, how it will affect them, how we will execute the decision, and other facts relevant to the situation. Essentially, I want to know everything about my various options. I want to understand what is likely to happen if I choose one path over another and what the alternatives may be. When I get as many facts and as much solid information as possible, I feel empowered to make a quality decision.

Step #3: Access the Experts

No one can better assist you in the decision-making process than an expert, someone who has deep experience and years of knowledge in the area pertaining to your decision. Your social circles, professional associations, and networks within your industry may include the experts you need. If not, those groups are certainly good places to ask for recommendations.

One caveat: I have learned that it's smart to gather multiple thoughts and opinions from experts and then sift through them. Unfortunately, some people may not share the whole truth, particularly if they are competitors in your industry or otherwise don't have your best interests at heart. Hopefully, you know people well enough to determine if they are honest, but thinking carefully and critically about the information you receive still makes sense.

I mentioned in an earlier chapter that when Dale and I started JRM, I spoke with the most knowledgeable people I knew. Some of those people were other race team owners, so we were all aware that we would compete against each other eventually. Because of my history in the sport, and because of things I'd heard my dad say, I had a good sense of whom I could trust. The experts I confided in were people who respected my dad and who respected Dale and me. Thankfully, they gave us good advice, even though we still wanted to beat each other on the track. But I like to think that they understood, as I do, that we can all help each other in appropriate ways, and that doing so raises the quality of competition, which ultimately benefits everyone involved.

When you are gathering information, it's important to recognize that everyone's opinion about a situation is related to their perception of the ultimate goal. Each person's experience will be different, particularly if the goal is different. Understanding your end goal, thinking through it, and communicating it clearly can make all the difference in terms of the advice you receive and the way you evaluate it.

For example, someone who is known as a "foodie" could tell you that XYZ restaurant is the best in town. But if XYZ is a seafood restaurant and you don't like fish, it will not be the best restaurant for you. Remember this analogy when accessing experts, and make sure you provide all the information they need to give you insight and information tailored to your specific needs and objectives.

In addition, the Internet makes looking up experts easy. Personally, I trust recommendations from people I know much more than the unknowns of the Internet, but there might be a time when your need for an expert is so specialized that the Internet is a good place to start. To be smart about finding experts online, be sure to look for a good number of verified reviews, not just three or four. The best thing about the Internet is it can help you formulate questions you can then take to experts you know to sift through whether the information online is accurate or not.

Step #4: Talk to the People the Decision Affects

The impact of a decision is rarely limited to the decision-maker; it often has a domino effect. In a professional setting, the decision might affect a department or even an entire organization. Personal decisions can affect friends, spouses, even entire families. Because the consequences of our decisions extend beyond ourselves, discussing them with the people they will affect is both wise and respectful.

You'll have greater support for the decisions you make if you take time to explain them to those who will be affected by their impact. The better they understand the issues and the more you can walk through any concerns or questions, the more accepting everyone will be.

I think we do this well at JRM. We hold weekly status meetings with multiple departments, which allow people from each area of the company to see the impact of what others are doing. It also gives them a chance to think about how something happening in another department might inspire them to engage their own team. We also have weekly managers' meetings during which we discuss potential decisions and what they would mean. This enables us to arrive at a perspective based on a team of eight or nine people, not one or two. During these discussions, someone often raises a point that the person who first brought up the issue has not thought about; this helps us work toward a decision. While we move quickly in many ways, I also want to make sure we don't rush into decisions until we have gained the clarity that can only come from thinking situations through, talking them out, and hearing various perspectives on them.

For example, let's say we need to make a decision about our company health insurance. This is the kind of issue we would discuss in a managers' meeting. We may start by stating that we need to trim the bottom line by moving to a different set of parameters for insurance. Then we begin talking about various considerations that should factor into our decision. We would ask, "How do our insurance premiums and the coverage we provide our employees compare to what our competitors offer?" This is an important question to ask from a recruiting and retention standpoint. We would continue asking questions until we arrived at what we considered the best decision.

When I see something that I feel might need to change, I gather the people involved and affected by it to talk it out. Once we understand the ramifications of various options, we move forward. This way of approaching decisions is more time-consuming than simply having me, or a few executives around me, make decisions on our own, but it serves our company well.

DECISIONS, DECISIONS

I have to make some type of significant decision at work every day. I also have decisions to make at home—what to cook for dinner, whether to let my children attend a social event, or when to plan a visit with my college-age daughter who lives out of town. The principles and steps for good decision-making I've discussed in this chapter are applicable both in the office and outside it.

Every day, from the time we get up until we go to bed, we make multiple decisions. Some are second nature, and we instinctively know what to do; others require considerable thought and time. In any case, the ability to make smart decisions has a huge impact on being able to achieve our goals, whether we're seeking professional success or personal achievement.

SEVEN

POSITION FOR SUCCESS

Behind my desk at JRM is a large window that runs almost the length of the room. When I look out of it, I do not see the mountains, creeks, or other scenic beauty of my home state of North Carolina; I see a race shop. I see busy mechanics and engineers fine-tuning elite racecars for another weekend on the track. In a way, the shop represents my highest ideal for our company.

In our race shop, everything—and I do mean *every* little thing, down to thousands of specific nuts, bolts, and other small pieces of hardware—has its place. You could walk into our shop right this minute and ask a crew member for a three-quarter-inch fine-thread bolt, and he could find it immediately. One of my goals for our organization is to be like the race shop—with every component in its proper place so we can function at our optimum.

Think about it this way: if someone uses a screw that is just one-sixteenth of an inch too small to attach parts to a racecar, big trouble—even disaster—could result. Just as the wrong screw in the wrong place could cause problems for a car on a track, a poorly placed employee can cause trouble in an organization. People who are not in the right places tend to be less engaged and productive, and they make more mistakes than those who are more engaged.

As a business owner, my components are not nuts and bolts; they're people. Part of my job is to make sure each person in our organization is in the right place—the place where they can thrive, operate out of their strengths, and be most productive as one element of the whole of our business. Ensuring that this happens is one way I can best position our company to accomplish what we need to do.

At JRM, as in many organizations, we have limited resources. One of my responsibilities is to be efficient with the resources available to me and to maximize the productivity of each one. For example, I have to cap our head count at a certain number in order to stay fiscally responsible. To use those resources efficiently, we need the best people working in the best places. Some companies have so many workers that they can overlook a few weaknesses in employees who do not carry their share of the load, but we can't do that. I need to know about those who don't fulfill their obligations or pull their weight, because I can't allow someone who is only doing a portion of a job to continue without demonstrating the will and ability to improve. I need every person on our team to be firing on all eight cylinders—maximum capacity—just like our racecars.

Achieving success is difficult if we've hired someone who simply is not right for a certain role. When team members are out of place, they tend to make mistakes and become inefficient because they find their jobs challenging or overwhelming instead of enjoyable. When that happens, other well-placed staff members almost always end up picking up the slack, and trust between colleagues begins to erode because someone cannot be counted on. Eventually, morale begins to suffer. Everyone ends up focusing on what's going wrong instead of building on what's going right. As a result, the manager spends too much time fixing situations that should not be broken.

I want a team in which every member is confident that the other members will do their parts to contribute to the success of the entire company and that they will do it with excellence. I want them to be empowered to think more about solutions than problems. Having the right people in the right places creates the efficient, productive, well-oiled machine that causes any business to thrive.

START EARLY

Putting the right people in the right places, positioning them for success, cannot start too soon. In fact, I began doing it before Dale and I officially left DEI. There was a lot I didn't know when I began building a viable business entity for my brother, but I did know I needed a solid plan. I didn't want to announce our new venture and then figure it out; I wanted to be ready to move full speed ahead the minute our plans became known. So as soon as I was certain of what we were going to do, I began speaking confidentially with the smartest people in our sport, people I identified because of their longevity and history of success.

What mattered greatly to me was not where these people *were*, but where they were *not*. I had to proceed carefully and discreetly. I couldn't talk to anyone employed by DEI, which eliminated some very knowledgeable people who could have provided important business insights they had learned from my dad.

Because I had developed relationships in NASCAR apart from Dad, and also because he enjoyed widespread admiration across the industry, I knew whom I could turn to for counsel regarding my new venture with Dale. There were enough people I trusted—and who understood the challenges Dale and I faced at DEI—for me to have a solid group of advisors to count on. Many of them had worked with my dad previously. They knew so much more than I did. I had a hunch they would be happy and eager to help us, and they were.

One of the first people I called was my boss at Sports Image, Joe Mattes. He is the man I consider to be the most knowledgeable person in NASCAR licensing. My initial conversation with Joe about an independent JRM took place during a meeting in March 2007, before Dale and I announced that we were leaving DEI. I tried to subtly let Joe know what we were thinking, so I asked him, "Do you know a VP of licensing who would want to work for me?"

He had no idea where I wanted to take the conversation, so after he made small talk about various licensing VPs he thought might be interested, I said, "Joe, let me be more clear about this. I'm not going public with this yet, but Dale and I are leaving DEI. We want everything buttoned up and ready to go before we announce it. We're going to bring all of his business in-house and build his brand. Are you interested in being our VP of licensing?"

"Yeah, I might be interested."

He then asked me about the timing, and I said, "Before the end of the year."

I called Joe several weeks after that conversation and officially asked him to come to work for us. He started in July 2007.

Joe gives me a lot of credit for setting the business up well, but one reason I was able to do that was that good people—such as Joe, Rick Hendrick, and others—were willing to help and support me from the start.

Joe recalled:

Kelley had the foresight to be prepared and to set everything up right from the very beginning. Back then—and to this day—she wants to know, "How do we do this right?" This is because she and Dale are proud of being the third generation of Earnhardt racers. It's a privilege and a responsibility they don't take lightly. The planning that took place before they launched JR Motorsports as a separate business entity was amazing. Kelley built a team that positioned us to succeed before we really got started. She had everything and everybody in place.

When she and Dale left DEI, all of NASCAR was shocked. When they announced it, it was like Kelley's coming-out party. She had driven a stake in the ground and said to everyone, "We got this." She wasn't cocky. She was just confident that she and Dale could build a better mousetrap, so to speak. And she had reason to be confident. She had surrounded herself with great people. She had done her homework. It was a daunting task, but she did it and she was ready.[1]

One of the best lessons I learned during this time was that I didn't have to know everything. I had to figure out what was truly important for *me* to know and what I could entrust to others. I maintain strong, open communication with the people I trust, and I can count on them to tell me what I need to know in order to run our organization most effectively. That has taken a great deal of pressure off of me as the person in charge. It has also helped free time and energy for me to focus on my family and other interests.

HIRE WISELY, TRAIN WELL

Not everyone has a chance to start their path toward winning in business early. Often, only those who begin a new business have a chance to craft it from its inception. Others inherit their companies, either literally, as in the case of family businesses, or because a previous leader has left the organization. Those who may not be able to start early can always apply the next lesson I have learned about positioning people to succeed, which is to develop good hiring and training practices.

Good hiring processes will enable you to select the candidate most closely matched with the job—not just in terms of that person's skill set but also in terms of personality, temperament, and attitude. When we interview candidates for open positions at JRM, we listen carefully for clues and insights into their personalities, work ethics, and other relevant qualities. Asking about various challenges or opportunities they could encounter and how they would handle those situations is very important. In addition, I ask them to give me real-world examples of circumstances they've dealt with in their previous employment. This gives me a good sense of what kind of person they are and helps me assess whether they can handle the role for which I am considering them.

Some of our best staff members are people I worked with before we started JRM. The reason I hired them is that I knew so much about them and their work ethics, their dedication, and their skills.

Obviously, those hires were easy, and those people have been loyal, long-term members of our team.

Hiring from a pool of candidates I have never met is more difficult than choosing from a group of people I know. The interview process is crucial to making a great decision, so I have trained myself to focus on making sure I ask candidates the right open-ended questions—instead of yes or no questions—to get them talking as much as possible. For example, instead of asking, "Have you ever had a situation in which such-and-such happened?" I say, "Tell me about a situation in which such-and-such happened." I don't ask a potential human resources employee if he or she has ever fired someone; I say, "How have you handled situations in which you've had to fire someone?" That helps me sift through the typical "good interviewees" and get to the hard workers with a skill set matched to the open position.

One hire that has worked out especially well is our accounting manager. The previous manager had been with us for ten years, and she still works off-site part-time as our tax accountant. She had a wealth of knowledge because of her longtime experience in the job—knowledge and insight that would not be transferrable to a new hire. Her position was a big role for me to fill.

During the interview process, what drew me to the candidate I chose for the role was her personality. She had a good skill set, but I felt she "fit" our organization in a way no other candidate did. She was outgoing, a little feisty, and fairly confident. She had also worked for other motorsports organizations, and I was able to get good, honest referrals from people in the industry.

My human resources director and I debated between this candidate and another person. I went with the one we hired, Denise, because the other candidate had the skills needed but her personality was a bit drier. Denise started with us in 2016 and is doing a great job. Sometimes we have to work to rein in the feistiness that drew me to her, but she is dedicated, gets the job done, and works to be the best. She is a good fit for us and an asset to our company.

I haven't always followed my instinct, put so much weight on personality, or heeded my intuition about how someone will fit into our organization. That's something I had to learn. I have definitely made a few hiring "fails" by choosing candidates with the most experience and good interview skills instead of taking risks on people with less experience but with a positive attitude and willingness to learn. In one situation, the candidate I chose lasted just one year; after that I hired the person I should have hired to begin with.

Once a candidate has been hired, offering a quality training process is vital to his or her success. This includes in-house training, but you should also make additional resources or classes available to help new hires perform better in their roles. This in-house training process usually involves sitting down with various departments and understanding what they do, how they work within the company, and how they interact with the team as a whole.

As I've mentioned, I think one of the most important qualities a person needs to succeed is a positive attitude and a willingness to work. Skills can be taught, but those attributes cannot. If I see a positive attitude and a strong work ethic, I'm comfortable sending people to classes and providing additional training to help them gain the skills they need or understand why their role is valuable to the organization.

The right training can take an employee's performance and contribution to the company to a new level. For example, just recently we needed to find a new manager for the Dale Jr. Foundation. Because I was aware of some changes coming in another area of our business, I knew the employees in that department would be looking for jobs. One of those employees had been with us for twelve years, and because of her tenure and dedication, I wanted to try to find a position for her under the JRM umbrella.

Her skills were solidly in the area of marketing, and she had no experience with nonprofit endeavors. But she knew the ins and outs of our company, and she also understood Dale's brand, so I felt she would be a great fit to lead the foundation. Still, she needed to learn more about nonprofits and why they operate the way they do, and she needed to understand the regulations that govern them. I found a good place to send her for training, and I spoke with her about my commitment to get her the help she needed to succeed in a new role. It has been a good fit. I'm glad I took the chance to use her skill set to benefit our foundation.

Both in the hiring process and in subsequent training, one of the most important things I can do is to honestly assess people's strengths and weaknesses—and, as in the case of our foundation manager, their potential. It's important to do this regularly to determine if people's strengths outweigh their weaknesses to the point that your organization gets what it needs from them.

Just as the needs of certain positions and job assignments change over time, people evolve too. Some people grow quickly as employees and can fill a variety of positions of increasing authority and responsibility, while others are better suited to stay in a certain role for an extended period of time or even for the duration of their work life. While upward mobility is generally positive, there is also something good to be said for an employee with great depth of experience and corporate history, one who loves the job and is faithful to it day in and day out. For example, we have all heard stories about engineers who thrive on hands-on work, then are promoted to management and find it stressful and unfulfilling. Once they leave that so-called promotion and get back to their old jobs, they're happy again. Climbing the career ladder is desirable for many people, but there will also always be a few who do best right where they are. Honest assessment will determine whom to move and where to move them but also whom to leave alone.

Being aware of people's strengths and weaknesses helps them utilize their skill sets to increase personal productivity and to benefit an entire department. I encourage managers to use every tool available to evaluate the people who keep their companies going each day.

At JRM, we use a program called "Management by Strengths" (MBS). According to their website, this is a program designed to help companies increase their productivity and "improve customer satisfaction and employee morale through an improved understanding of how to work more effectively together."[2] The test assigns people a certain color according to their dominant traits—directness (red), extroversion (green), pace (blue), and structure (yellow). By knowing a person's color and the colors of others they work with, we can better understand our employees. If we hit a roadblock, the program helps us identify why people operate the way they do and how we can approach or manage them differently to get the best results.

In our race shop hangs a whiteboard. Everyone who works for us, including me, has a colored line on this board that identifies his or her temperament, so it's easy to get a sense of who each employee is. For example, the program identifies me as a "high direct" person.

I am straightforward and to the point, and I want results! When everyone on the team knows how to best communicate with one another, we work together more effectively to get the best results. When all the individual relationships run smoothly, the whole organization is better.

One of the best things I've done along these lines in my personal life is to study the book *The Five Love Languages* by Gary Chapman, with L.W. We discovered that my love languages are gifts and acts of service, while his is affection. Because we know this, he understands that birthday gifts and Christmas presents are important to me, as is making my coffee in the morning. I know that he feels loved when I give him hug, an unexpected kiss, or a meaningful touch.

Making the effort to understand people so we can better relate to them—both at work and in our personal lives—benefits everyone.

BE OPEN TO NEW IDEAS

The final key point I want to mention about positioning for success is to be open to new ideas, things that have never been tried in your organization—or at least not tried in a long time.

If there was ever anyone who might be considered the right person in the right place, it's my brother Dale. After all, our father and grand-father were racers. Dale is not only my dad's namesake but also seemed to be the natural heir to everything my dad built in professional sports. People think my dad groomed Dale to become a professional racecar driver and to carry on his legacy. They believe that from the time Dale was born, he was destined to win NASCAR races.

But as I noted earlier, when Dale and I were young, Dad never seemed to want him to drive, and he didn't train or encourage him to become the next great Earnhardt racecar driver. Nevertheless, Dale started racing Late Model cars in Myrtle Beach, South Carolina, in 1991. He completed 159 races and won only 4. Dad never went to see him drive, never asked about his races, and never offered any direction or encouragement to help Dale perform better.

At the end of 1997, Dale ran out of money and thought his racing career was finished. He walked into one of Dad's shops one day and saw what we would now call an Xfinity Series car with his name painted on it. Thinking people were playing a mean joke on him, he was angry. He knew that if Dad had decided to let him race for DEI, he would have told him, right?

Well, Dad did choose to put Dale behind the wheel, but it wasn't his idea, and he didn't tell him. One of my dad's crew chiefs at DEI was also one of his best friends—my mom's brother, our uncle Tony, known to us as Tony Sr. Putting Dale in that car was Tony Sr.'s idea. He basically said to my dad one day, "You're spending a lot of money putting young guys in your cars. Why don't you invest some of it in your own son?"

The right person to carry on Dad's racing legacy—his own son—was right in front of him for years, yet Dad could not see it. In order to get Dale in the right place, Dad had to open his mind to the idea that Dale could drive. Thankfully, he did, and the guys in the shop prepared the car for Dale. Dale walked into the shop and saw the car before Dad ever said anything about it. When he realized it was not a joke, he was beyond excited.

Dale finally found his niche when he started driving in the Xfinity Series. He was the right person in the right place, and he won the championship in 1998 and again in 1999.

Dale says his relationship with our dad changed immediately when he began driving for DEI. They did begin talking more about racing then, but they also began to engage with each other personally, and the father-son bond Dale always longed for began to take shape. For the two of them, Dale remembered, "Those three years—1998, 1999 and 2000—were as good as it could get."[3]

Once my brother got into the right place, there was no stopping him. Until he retired in 2017, the right place for Dale Earnhardt Jr. was behind the wheel of a racecar. I wish my dad had figured that out sooner and encouraged him to be a racer earlier in his life. Had Dad done that when Dale was a child and a teenager, the two of them could have had more time to enjoy a better relationship. We had no way of knowing that their time as father and son would be cut short. The synergy between them, which was in its infancy when our dad died, could have become truly amazing, not only for my dad and Dale but for NASCAR and fans all over the world.

Be diligent about putting the right people in the right places. Sometimes that comes easily. You can interview a candidate and sense intuitively how that person will fit into your company. You know where he or she belongs, and you feel certain that having that individual in place will be positive for the company. Other times, something tells you a candidate is capable of grasping the corporate vision and could quickly become an asset. That's when you get creative about looking for a place for that potential employee—perhaps as a special assistant to a department manager, as an independent contractor, or as a part-time employee until a full-time position becomes available.

I'm thankful that today Dale and I are both in the right places where our strengths are maximized. We are happier, and so is our entire team. In the same way, whatever you have to do to get the right people in the right places so they and your organization can succeed, do it. The benefits will put you in the winner's circle every time.

EIGHT

LET GO TO MOVE FORWARD

In the professional racing industry, moving forward is literally what keeps us going. If our cars don't move forward faster than those belonging to other teams, our business suffers. If they do, we thrive. All businesses have to move forward in order to stay strong and to grow, and that starts with leadership. An organization can't move beyond the vision of the person or team at the top.

But moving forward is not enough; we also have to intentionally let go of what holds us back. To use an analogy, a driver would be foolish to push the accelerator to the floor while staring in the rearview mirror. Nothing good could come of that. Instead, a driver has to choose to look ahead and then take off in that direction. The victory is in front of him, not behind him. The same is true for you.

All kinds of situations can keep us from moving forward, both personally and professionally. When something significant hinders us from moving ahead personally, such as adversity or tragedy, it affects our lives at work—even if we try hard not to let it. Professionally, policy revisions or rule changes, leadership changes, or market fluctuations in the industry can cause momentum to cease. Unexpected expenses or budget crises can result in a standstill. Personality conflicts among leadership or team members—the way people feel about working with others—can keep an organization from making progress. But ultimately, whatever slows us down or grinds us to a halt is usually more in our minds than in our circumstances. Negative thought processes and attitudes can make us stagnant, while positive thinking can generate forward motion even in the face of difficult realities. I've found that the most helpful mind-set when facing situations that prevent us from moving ahead is to simply let them go.

People let go of things for different reasons and in different ways. Sometimes they let go because they trust God. I definitely seek wisdom from God in the Bible and through prayer, and I trust Him to lead me in the right way. People who do not relate to a being beyond themselves may let go because they've tried everything they know and failed so much that they don't want to try again. Others let go because they find new ventures or other ways to use their energy. And some people simply don't have the energy or ability to care anymore. They give up, which is much different from letting go.

Sometimes, as was the case for Dale and me at DEI, people let go for complicated reasons beyond their control. We certainly had the strength to continue caring about Dad's company, but we had exhausted every possible avenue to remain part of it in a healthy way. We had worked as hard as we could for as long as we could, and we could see that Dale's career would never move forward as it needed to under the leadership of the people there. Someone else's hands would always be on the gearshift.

Things that will not move us forward serve no purpose in our future. Sure, we can and should view them as learning experiences, but once we've learned the lessons they teach us, we need to walk away from them and refuse to allow them to influence us anymore. That's one of the freeing, empowering decisions we can make.

BUILDING SOMETHING NEW AFTER ADVERSITY

One of my first big tests as a business leader presented itself before I ever took the helm at JRM, when I realized that no one at DEI was looking out for Dale's best interests and that his moving forward with them would benefit them while hurting him. This realization, along with the decision to let go of my dad's company, was personally painful.

I've always been proud of the Earnhardt name and the Earnhardt legacy. Part of what drives me every day is upholding what our family name means to NASCAR and beyond. To think that Dale and I could be involved in our sport apart from our dad's name was sad, disappointing, and emotionally grueling. We were deeply attached to our family business, so before we could move forward, we had to think objectively about it. We had to ask what would take us to the next step, and DEI was not the answer. The logical side of me—the businesswoman—*knew* that Dale and I had to move on, but my heart struggled with the idea for quite some time. That's one reason we tried so hard to hold on before we finally let go.

Although we still respected and appreciated Richard Childress Racing, we had also reached the point where we didn't feel we needed to try to honor our dad by partnering with them. We had to do something different, something right for us. The course we wanted to chart moving forward didn't include maintaining any particular tie to the past.

We are happy and thankful to still have a good relationship with Richard. He is one of our biggest supporters, and we call him a friend. When JRM started racing in the Xfinity Series in 2006, we leased our engines from Richard. But when we merged in 2008 with Hendrick Motorsports, we switched to Hendrick engines. I think Richard understood and respected Dale's position not to follow in Dad's shadows any more than was necessary.

Richard knew our dad better than anyone, and he knows first-hand some of the unique challenges and personality conflicts we faced at DEI. He tells us that our dad would be proud to this day of what we have done, the decisions we have made, and how we have handled ourselves and our business.

Sometimes the hardest things to let go of are the adversities we encounter or the results or consequences of those difficult times. Adversity is usually considered bad, so we might think people are eager to leave negative circumstances behind them. Not always—sometimes adversity has a fierce grip on us because it ties us to a situation or a person that was meaningful. For Dale and me, the last ties we had with our dad were the adversity of his death and the attempts we made to stay connected to him through DEI. We knew his legacy would always flow through our veins and live in our hearts, but we wanted more than that.

I learned through that situation that finding the courage to let go and build something new after tragedy is a unique journey, but a vital one. Nothing can keep us from moving forward like adversity can, so letting go of it on purpose is essential to good leadership. I realize that it's not always easy; sometimes it's difficult and painful. But if holding on will hold you back, then letting go is always best.

MOVING ON IS A BIG MOVE

One of the hardest letting-go decisions I've made in my personal life was to move away from my mom and Dale. For many years, all of us lived close to each other on adjoining property in Mooresville, North Carolina. After I married L.W. and we had a child of our own, I sensed we needed a different living arrangement. Nothing specific happened to cause me to want to put distance between my birth family and the one L.W. and I share. There was no argument, nothing to upset the way we had all been living for so long. In fact, thinking about living more than just a few minutes from my mom and Dale was difficult. I love them, and I enjoyed having them close. But the time came when we knew our family needed to move forward to establish our own homeplace. We dreamed of a plot of land for ourselves, a spot on earth that belonged just to us.

L.W. is an avid outdoorsman, and he and I both liked the idea of having a large piece of land and a small lake surrounded by woods. Although thinking about not having my birth family nearby was painful, we started looking for our own property. We took our time to make a good decision and found exactly what we wanted, a truly perfect place for our family.

Well, the *property* was ideal. The *house* needed significant updating! That's complete now, and we've ended up with a peaceful retreat that we and our children love to call home—about twenty miles from where we lived previously.

After I moved, I was surprised to find that Dale, Mom, and I seemed to love each other more than ever. When L.W. and I decided to move, Dale was just days away from marrying his wife, Amy, so dynamics were changing for everyone. We used to be able to drop in on each other any time. Now we live thirty minutes away, so Dale and I are intentional about planning ahead to visit each other. I think my family's move has been a net gain for everyone. Letting go of the living arrangement that had been comfortable for so long was not easy, but it was right.

FINDING THE COURAGE TO LET GO

When I was very young, before the Internet and social media took off, one of the most popular syndicated news columnists in America was Ann Landers. People from all over the world wrote letters to her about their problems, and she responded with advice. People considered her a smart woman, and if she said something, many regarded it as true. I definitely think what she said about letting go is accurate: "Some people believe holding on and hanging in there are signs of great strength. However, there are times when it takes much more strength to know when to let go and then do it."[1]

Letting go takes not only strength but also courage. Many times we refuse to let go even when we know something isn't good for us, because it's familiar. It's comfortable. If we no longer cling to that—whether it's a business model, a relationship, a way of thinking, a system of time management, or an attitude toward coworkers—we'll be left without that sense of comfort. We'll have to do something new and different, something unproven. There are no guarantees that the new way will work. It's risky.

One of the biggest risks I've taken—and one of the most painful decisions I've made as a business owner—involved a family member who worked for JRM. My uncle, Tony Sr., held an important position as our competition director. He was the one who encouraged our dad to let Dale race for him, and he had worked as Dale's crew chief in the early days of Dale's professional career. After five seasons in that role, our teams simply weren't winning, so we took the difficult step of letting him go. At the time, Dale said in an interview with ESPN, "I can't think of anyone who has impacted my career and development as a driver more than Tony Sr."[2]

Here's the heartfelt statement I issued:

> I believe Tony Sr.'s passion for the sport is exceeded only by his yearning to excel in it, and that itself became the issue that both he and I struggled with. At JR Motorsports we do this to win races and compete for championships, and lately we have not met that standard. Being the competitor that Tony Sr. is, I know that bothers him more than anyone.[3]

Tony Sr.'s son, our cousin Tony Jr., also worked for us as a crew chief, and soon after Tony Sr.'s departure, we let him go too. These were two industry veterans with long histories of success, but for some reason their previous success did not translate to JRM, and they were not moving us forward. The time came when I had to let them go so they could find a place where they could be successful and so we could move into what we needed to do to find the wins we were looking for.

Those decisions were risky and painful, but ultimately they were good, and we don't regret them. We didn't make them lightly. I certainly thought them through because I wanted to be wise in leading our company. Generally speaking, people in leadership positions aren't risk averse. Most often, to reach their positions they have taken chances in their professional lives. But the best leaders don't embrace every risk that presents itself. They assess the risk, evaluate the potential reward, and move forward with the right combination of boldness and wisdom.

More than once I've had to move on personally after letting a family member go professionally. I've learned to focus on the personal aspects of the relationship and leave the work situation at work. Once you've had the conversation about termination at work, let that be the end of the matter. There's no need to bring up the situation again. The professional issue is behind you, and both people need to let it end while moving forward as much as possible as family members. People can be a poor fit for your business environment but still be very valuable in your family.

You have to let go of yesterday because it doesn't take you toward tomorrow. In her book *Healing the Soul of a Woman*, bestselling author Joyce Meyer wrote this about letting go:

> Letting go involves making a commitment to stop thinking about what people have done to you, unless of course, you are receiving counseling or sharing your victory over it in order to help someone else. Sometimes people replay moments of betrayal, abuse, or rejection over and over in their minds, and whether they know it or not, doing so holds them in bondage to it. Our minds affect our emotions, and when we rehearse abusive

events over and over, it brings back the original pain as if it were a current event.[4]

No one wants to bring back pain as though it is a current event. That alone should inspire the courage to let go. If you sense you need to let go of something in order to move forward and are looking for the strength and courage to do it, here are several simple questions to ask yourself:

- If I let go, what's the worst that could happen? Could I live with that?
- If I let go, what's the best that could happen? How much do I want that?
- If I let go, am I (or is our company) willing and positioned to make the adjustments—perhaps the sacrifices—necessary to embrace the best that could happen?
- If I don't let go, where will I (or my organization) be six months from now, two years from now, ten years from now? How much will I regret being held back?

These questions may not be typical, as some assess risk only in financial terms. They calculate what the risk will cost and how much it could affect the bottom line, and that kind of evaluation is necessary. We do have to think about dollars and cents. But people who want to win in business and in life challenge themselves to think about these kinds of intangibles, realizing that if there is a longing in their drive to take their organizations or their personal situations in a certain direction, that drive will not be satisfied until it happens.

IF YOU CAN'T CONTROL IT . . .

I recently posted on my Facebook page: "Don't worry about what you can't control." Joyce Meyer expanded on the same point this way: "Don't keep holding on to something you cannot do anything about. If someone hurt you badly and you hang onto it mentally and emotionally, then you are allowing it to keep hurting you day after day. Help yourself and let it go!"[5]

Control is a necessary component of business and life. In business, leaders have a lot of control—the last word, in fact—over many things, but not over everything. They control the high-level decisions that affect their employees and perhaps entire industries. They control budgets, schedules, policies, and all sorts of important matters. But, I repeat, they do not control everything. Many leaders find it very frustrating that certain people and situations are simply out of their reach. They think, *If I could just get involved and change certain situations, everything would turn out well. I could fix this!*

Striving to manage what we can't control is a huge hindrance to moving forward. It occupies our minds and keeps us from thinking productively; it wastes our energy; it takes us nowhere. Those situations influence us, often in negative ways, yet we cannot influence them at all. So we have to make a choice: Will we continue to use our mental and emotional strength trying to change them, or will we let them go?

I spent much of my life wishing I could control my stepmother, Teresa, but I couldn't. I wanted her to treat Dale and me better when we were young, but I had no power to make her do that. By the time Dale and I were adults, I still wanted her to treat us better professionally, but I couldn't do it. Finally accepting that and making peace with it so I could move forward was one of the most freeing decisions I've ever made. I'm now in a place where I would be open to a healthy relationship with her, and part of the way I reached this point was to let go of everything I could not control.

The first part of the well-known Serenity Prayer, written by American theologian Reinhold Niebuhr, says, "God, grant me the serenity to accept the things I cannot change, the courage to change the things I can, and the wisdom to know the difference."[6] I think we can substitute the word *control* for *change* in this prayer.

Anyone who wants to win needs to know what they can control, what they cannot control, and the difference between the two. There will always be people who do things, say things, and make decisions that affect us. When the impact is positive, we can celebrate. When we're unable to control situations—whether it's a negative social media post from a disgruntled employee, market volatility that impacts our bottom line, an unexpected turn of events for a valuable player on our team, a challenge in our personal lives, or a seemingly unresolvable conflict—we're wise to accept it, put it behind us, and move forward.

FREE TO MOVE FORWARD

Letting go turned a tragedy into a point of redemption in my life. My dad's death was devastating. That alone could have stopped me from moving forward, at least for a season, had I let it. I could have stayed stuck in that place for a long time. I had to let go of the grief, the unfulfilled desires, and the hope of working under his name. I had to learn that letting go of these things didn't mean forfeiting my dad's legacy. I can still carry it on. Letting go enabled me to do that on my terms, not anyone else's.

God had a plan for my life beyond my father's accident. While his absence in my life will always be painful, I truly feel that if my dad had not passed away and Dale and I had not been willing to let go of DEI, I would never have had the opportunity to do what I do today—lead an amazing group of people in a family environment, in a healthy, vibrant corporate culture, in a sport I love. That connection with people is so close to my heart, and the relationship I have with our employees is special. Today Dale and I are building a new legacy while also carrying Dad's legacy forward, and our employees are part of what gives us the opportunity to do what we love. Sharing all of that with the JRM team is a privilege and a joy. In the wake of adversity, had I not learned to let go of the circumstances beyond my control, I would not have been able to move beyond the past into the life I now enjoy.

I would like to close this chapter with a question and some encouragement: What are you holding on to that is preventing you from taking the next step? Whatever it is, ask yourself if it is valuable enough to hold you back. The only way to make room for what will propel you into the future is to let go of what holds you in the past. Summon the courage to let go and see what kinds of amazing things happen once you are free to move forward.

NINE

CUSTOMIZE YOUR COMMUNICATION

Former presidential speechwriter and author James Humes said, "The art of communication is the language of leadership."[1] He's right—the ability to communicate effectively is one of the key skills that empower a leader to actually lead, to get things done. Without it, a leader can end up creating confusion and even chaos in his or her organization. The same principle applies to our personal lives. If we can't communicate well, we won't make much progress toward our dreams.

People in leadership roles are intimately familiar with the various logistical elements of their companies—budgets, schedules, contracts, forecasts, technology, administration, and other activities specific to certain industries. For me, those specific elements include racecars, parts, transportation trucks, marketing and public relations materials, and licensing agreements.

Do you see what all of these have in common? None is a human being.

The human component is part of what makes each company

unique, and it's often what separates mediocre ones from good ones, and good ones from great ones. No matter how amazing a product is—whether it's a racecar or a tube of toothpaste—it can never rise above the abilities of the humans who created it. The people behind a product cannot do and be all they are supposed to do and be without effective communication.

This saying is one I have to laugh about because I know it's true: "The single biggest problem in communication is the illusion that it has taken place."[2] Sometimes we think we're communicating when we really aren't. We are talking or sending emails, but they aren't producing the results we need. Great communication moves a process forward; it does not allow anything to stall or move backward.

Libraries, magazines, and the Internet are full of advice on how to communicate effectively. Entire books have been written on that subject. My goal in this chapter is not to repeat information that's already available; instead, I want to share with you general principles of effective communication. Then I will focus specifically on learning to communicate effectively when dealing with conflict.

GREAT COMMUNICATION
UNDERSTANDS THE AUDIENCE

I've come to realize the importance of learning how your employees hear or read your communication and then tailoring your message to their style. When new employees join our company, one of the first tasks we ask them to complete is their Management by Strengths profile, because it's a great tool to help everyone know how to communicate most effectively with each other. For example, some people need direct, concise communication, and others need details and background information.

Just as you communicate differently with a spouse than you do with a sibling, you speak differently with various members of your professional team as well. Next time you get ready to share something important, regardless of the audience, these three simple questions can help your communication become more effective:

What Do They Already Know?

If people already know something, there's no need to repeat it. For example, everyone at JRM knows we will be racing at every event on the calendar. A complete schedule for the racing season hangs on a whiteboard in our shop so everyone can see it, and many conversations around the office pertain to upcoming races. I don't need to tell anyone when the Daytona season opener is; they already know.

Instead of rehashing what's already common knowledge, simply reference it as needed and then move on to make your point. You can do so quickly with a sentence such as "With the Daytona 500 coming up in February . . ."

What Needs Additional Clarification?

One reason progress slows in many organizations is that people are informed but confused. This is usually the result of a communication breakdown at some point in the process. Occasionally you might think people know what to do simply because you've asked them to do it. That is not always the case; sometimes they need additional information or direction. Confusion often results when people are given a specific assignment without the context of a broader goal. In those cases, the only clarity needed is for them to understand how their role fits into a larger initiative.

What Do They Need to Know to Take the Next Step?

The best way to empower people to do what needs to be done is to make sure they have all the information they need to do it. This could include details as simple as a clear deadline: "I'll need this report by EOB on February 1." It could also involve more comprehensive instructions, such as "Form a team of six people to study the potential impact of this decision and meet weekly for a month to discuss it. Then give me a recommendation."

The test of whether or not our attempts to communicate are successful is this: Do they cause others to take the actions we need them to take? Truly effective communication moves a process forward.

GREAT COMMUNICATION FOCUSES ON FACTS, NOT FEELINGS

Generally speaking in business, the more we stick to facts and leave out feelings, the more effective our communication will be. Feelings do not normally enable communication that moves people toward getting things done; facts do.

Not long ago I needed to conduct a performance review for an employee. To my surprise, she asked to write her own review. I wondered if she might end up giving me a story about how much she loved her job (I hoped) or maybe how and why she struggled with certain parts of it. In other words, I was curious to see if her review might be more emotional and less objective than I needed it to be. But she seemed to be a smart, valuable employee, and her idea was so intriguing to me that I agreed to let her do it.

When I read it, I saw nothing but facts. Many of the sentences in her assessment began with the words "I did . . ." By the time I finished the report, I could clearly see that she was indeed as smart and as valuable an employee as I expected her to be. The unorthodox review process was positive because she understood that I needed to see facts and measurable results, and she communicated them clearly.

The employee didn't waste my time making statements about how she felt. She simply reported what she had done, offering one example after another to substantiate her claims, and I couldn't argue with that. She made a case for her value based on specific examples and a facts-based assessment of her accomplishments. Her communication was terrific, and it helped her reach her goal of a pay increase.

COMMUNICATING EFFECTIVELY DURING CONFLICT

For many people, the most difficult form of communication is communication during conflict. I don't know anyone who is eager to see conflict, but great leaders understand that disagreement, when it happens between two entities who are passionate, can make a company (or, in your personal life, a relationship) stronger. William Wrigley said, "In business, when two people always agree, one of them is irrelevant."[3]

Conflict that is about a person or an ego doesn't serve anyone well. But I believe in embracing conflict that happens as a part of positive growth and change. I also admit that dealing with conflict isn't pleasant. At JRM we do it as best we can; and we do our best to make it a stepping-stone, not a stumbling block, to the next level of greatness we want our organization to reach.

People may react in surprising ways when a conflict arises. Those who normally seem outgoing and talkative may suddenly withdraw from communicating. Those who seem quiet and reserved may find their voice and speak up, especially if they feel they've been violated or treated unfairly. This is because conflict pushes people into an entirely new realm of communicating. Making small talk with friends, coworkers, bosses, or employees around the break room or over lunch requires a "gift for gab," but dealing with differences of opinion or with volatile issues demands a completely different set of skills and priorities.

As happens in any healthy company, I empower managers to handle conflict between employees, and I expect them to do so. Anytime a conflict arises, employees know to go to their immediate supervisor about it before escalating it to anyone in a higher position on our organizational chart. If the immediate supervisor doesn't handle the situation to the employee's satisfaction, they can move to the next supervisory level. If at any point during the situation others need to get involved, the supervisor may call in a representative from human resources. Once a matter reaches human resources, someone has made me aware of it, and I usually need to address or mediate it.

By the time a conflict gets to me, emotions are usually high, especially if strong personalities and strong feelings factor into it. So the first step I take is what I've already noted—to put emotion aside. If I allow myself to feel too passionately about the issue, especially if the conflict involves a person or situation close to my heart, I may not assess it accurately. Besides, the people involved typically have enough emotion about the situation without having me get emotional about it too! My job is to bring peace and diffuse the situation, not to intensify it.

Next, I gather as much information as possible. I talk to each party involved individually so I can hear everyone's perspective. I ask them exactly what they think the problem is, because I know each person will view it and articulate it differently. The better I can understand how they interpret the problem, the better I can think through how to lead everyone to a resolution. Some people are able to talk about a problem objectively and clearly, while others tend to use feeling words and talk emotionally. Regardless of how they communicate, my goal is to encourage them to focus on facts and use concrete examples to articulate what they see as the bottom-line issue.

This is important to understand because the parties are not always willing to tell "the whole truth and nothing but the truth," due to their desire to protect themselves or someone else. These dynamics are tough because, as a manager and leader, I have to put together all the information I have with the understanding that I may not have been told accurately everything I need to know.

A good barometer for truth, almost a sixth sense to know when people are or are not being honest, is an important quality to have. We all want to be surrounded by honest people, but we occasionally find out that we are not. Sometimes circumstances or further developments vindicate those who are honest or indict those who are not. Sometimes intuition tells us certain people are telling the truth, while others are not. Sometimes coworkers, vendors, or others inadvertently provide us with insight that lets us know the truth. Sometimes dishonest people trip themselves up and we catch them in a lie, which can ultimately lead us to the truth.

As a problematic situation unfolds, nothing serves us better than asking the right questions of the right people—asking for details, examples, and cold, hard facts. I try to contain conflict to the fewest possible number of people because having too many aware of a problem is bad for morale and can create gossip. At the same time, I don't hesitate to ask anyone who knows about the problem to provide me with information I believe I need.

Given the size of our company and our family-oriented, all-in atmosphere, I bring everyone in together face-to-face when I can't get where I need to by talking to people individually. I start the conversation by setting up the situation and the facts as I have heard them. From there, we discuss a solution and give each person at the table the opportunity to offer his or her input. If people were not honest previously, that usually becomes evident and the truth comes out. In most cases we end up in a good place, having learned how we could have avoided the scenario that unfolded and how to keep it from happening again.

Recently I learned a lesson from a conflict at JRM: if I (yes, I) had copied a member of the team on an email, we could have avoided a problematic situation with another department in our company. The problem started with me, and I took ownership of that. My staff could have brought the other department into the discussion, but that didn't happen. Next time I'll make sure all parties are copied from the beginning.

No matter the conflict, I live by three values: Be honest. Be respectful. Be professional. Let's look at each one.

Be Honest

The only way to get to the bottom of any conflict is to talk about it forthrightly and openly. Some people avoid speaking honestly to protect themselves or others, to hide a mistake or failure, or to avoid looking like they can't do their job. Honesty requires trust. I do my best to earn and build the trust of my team and of people in my personal life because being trustworthy is the right thing to do and because when they trust me, they will tell me the truth.

I believe I have a responsibility to model the qualities I want in our team at JRM. I'm the leader, so I need to set the example. I don't want to hold the people around me to a higher standard than the one to which I hold myself. I can't expect them to give me anything—such as honesty—if I don't give it to them first.

In *Tao Te Ching*, the philosopher Lao Tzu wrote, "I am honest to those who are honest. And am also honest to those who are not honest. Thus is honesty attained."[4] He's right: not everyone we deal with will be honest, but that's no excuse for us to compromise the truth. Our job as leaders and as people is to be honest with everyone.

I want to offer one caveat: not everyone in an organization needs to know everything. That's why there are tiers of management. In some cases, leaders have knowledge that could help resolve a conflict, but sharing that knowledge simply to solve a problem between two employees would not be wise. In moments like that, being honest can be a challenge—but that's no excuse to compromise. We can find ways to tell the truth without disclosing information to people who do not need to know it or cannot be trusted with it.

Be Respectful

Most people can handle being disagreed with if they feel respected. Be courteous, speak kindly, and give others a chance to communicate what they need or want to say. Respect involves a willingness to truly hear what another person is saying and consider what that person thinks.

As a child and a young adult, I rarely felt heard and didn't feel that I mattered. I did not feel respected. That's one reason I want respect to be a key part of our corporate culture at JRM. It's important to me that each person on our team feels that he or she has a voice worth listening to, is able to speak, and expects to be heard. As the leader, I may not agree with everything employees say, but I respect them enough to listen without interruption and without judgment. Even if I disagree with or correct them, I do that with kindness and do my best to leave the person feeling respected.

In my personal life, instead of simply *telling* my children what to do, I *ask* them and explain why it's important. With my older children, I try to let them know I have heard them before offering my opinion. I don't discount what they say but respond by saying something like, "I can see how you felt that way, but have you thought about this . . . ?" I also try to be respectful in my choice of words when communicating with my family by using words such as *please* and *thank you.*

I once read an observation that 10 percent of conflicts are due to difference in opinion and 90 percent are due to wrong tone of voice. I don't know whether those statistics are accurate, but I do know that in most conflicts there's a real issue and a perceived issue. A true disagreement may exist, while the heart of the problem may not be the argument but the attitude one person perceives from the other. If a person feels disrespected, conflict probably isn't far behind. If I can help both parties treat each other with respect, the conflict or difference of opinion is usually easier to resolve.

Be Professional

Racing, like many sports, includes various levels of competition. Amateurs race for fun and may earn a little money doing it, but they are not professionals. Professionals are those disciplined enough, trained enough, and skilled or gifted enough to devote their lives to the sport as a career and to earn enough money to live well because of it. Professionals are the best of the best, and more is expected of them than of amateurs.

This is also true in the workplace. Even if the culture at your office is relaxed, standards of professionalism apply in behavior. Professionalism includes honesty and respect. It also includes being prepared to discuss a matter when the time comes, just as we would be prepared to make a presentation at a meeting. Professionalism involves the discipline to deal with disagreement in a way that keeps it focused on the matter at hand and not on secondary issues. It seeks to resolve conflicts as thoroughly as possible, but also as quickly as possible so everyone can get back to work. Because conflicts can be emotionally intense, they can easily spiral into pettiness or unfounded accusations. Professionalism doesn't let that happen.

Professionalism keeps the level of conversation high, not allowing the parties involved to take cheap verbal shots at each other, to scream or rant, or to resort to name-calling or inappropriate language; a conflict within a business is not a bar fight. Professionalism requires one to be reasonable, respectful, focused, and productive.

To resolve a conflict in a professional manner, all parties have to keep the organization's best interest, not their personal agendas, in mind. They also should avoid bringing up past problems that have already been resolved. If the conflict has deep roots, sorting it out may involve dealing with unresolved situations, but mentioning previous problems for the sake of stirring up trouble is not helpful or professional.

Conflict is unavoidable, but treating everyone involved with honesty, respect, and professionalism—and requiring them to deal with each other the same way—enables me to make great progress toward a resolution with maximum benefits.

Both at work and in other areas of life, effective communication is foundational to success. No matter whom we speak with or what the subject may be, the ability to clearly articulate information or opinions will contribute to a positive outcome.

TEN

AIM FOR THE WIN-WIN

At JRM, our entire business depends on winning. NASCAR is first and foremost a competitive professional sport. Without competition, our industry would cease to exist. Everything we do is driven by performance.

In a racecar, handling is everything. An adjustment of just one millimeter or an eighth of an ounce can make the difference between victory and defeat. Each racetrack is different, so part of our job is to understand the specific factors that can affect a car's performance and make sure our car handles those conditions as well as possible. We employ people in our shop with high levels of expertise, and we require them to work at a high level of precision. We send more than thirty people to each race, so working for us involves a heavy travel schedule for certain employees. They work hard. They work smart. They work fast. And they work with a hunger to win. So when our teams perform better than anyone else, I want our behind-the-scenes people to share in the excitement, to be recognized for their individual roles in our corporate success, and to be rewarded for their efforts and commitment to making us great.

In our business, people can become easily discouraged if we aren't winning. Competitors are like that. While every smart business operates with a competitive edge, that edge may be sharper in professional sports than in any other industry. Winning gives us an emotional boost we wouldn't trade for anything. That's why every win calls for a celebration at JRM.

We celebrate our wins on Mondays or Tuesdays, which are our busiest days as we prepare cars to leave the shop on Wednesdays for the next race. We often host a "Win Breakfast" or a "Win Lunch" for our staff, provided by our team sponsors, but we *always* have a victory celebration we call a "beer toast," which is most of our employees' favorite celebration.

JRM started small in the racing world in 2002, while still under the DEI umbrella. We didn't begin Xfinity racing until 2006. That year, Dale was sponsored by Budweiser, so it seemed fitting for our win celebrations to involve a beer toast. It has become a ritual for us.

Everyone joins the winning driver, the winning crew, me, and occasionally Dale, if his schedule permits. I give the driver and crew chief a chance to talk about the race. They talk about the weekend and thank everyone who worked to make it possible; then we raise a beer or glass of water to toast the victory, and all of us ring a bell. The bell is significant because Rick Hendrick is one of the owners of JRM, and Hendrick Motorsports has a tradition of ringing a bell to celebrate their wins. We hung a victory bell in our shop as a way of tying the two entities together and as a nod of respect and appreciation to Mr. Hendrick. Sure, it can get a little loud, but everyone enjoys it.

Next, I call the name of each employee and personally give a win sticker to every one of them, along with a handshake and a comment such as "Way to go!" In any group of people, the shy ones tend to stay toward the back of the gathering. To avoid anyone not being recognized, I ask everyone to stand in a circle, where I can see everyone's faces. I make comments focused on helping everyone transition from hard-at-work mode to the celebration of their accomplishments. We are a lean group of focused professionals, and if I can help us all relax for a few minutes before getting back to work, that's good.

On special occasions, we give our staff gifts representing key races or milestones. I try to make sure our gifts represent the specific race to which they are tied. For example, there's a group of four races called Dash 4 Cash. If any team wins all four, they receive $1 million. The winner of each individual race receives $100,000. One year, we won three of the four races. Since we did well in the Dash 4 Cash, the gift that seemed appropriate to me was, well, cash! I handed out $100 bills at that win celebration. Another time, we won a trophy shaped like a huge gas station pump, a nod to the race's sponsor. That particular win was JRM's fortieth, so we gave our employees gas cards worth $40 each.

As is the case for any team, we have great years and we have off years. In 2010, we had a very difficult and discouraging year, but in 2014, 2017, and 2018 we won championships. My job is to find ways to guide us toward more great years and to steer us wisely through the years that don't go well.

Our win celebrations are just one more way I try to be approachable, effective, and involved as a leader. Everybody loves a win and every win deserves a celebration. Employees who feel valued and celebrated over one win become motivated to win again.

Winning is in my blood. I'm not sure I would even know how to think as a businesswoman if I took winning out of the equation! But I understand that if a win is *only* about those at the top, it feels like an empty victory. I believe that there's more than enough winning to go around. In my personal life and in business, I want to do everything I can do to win and to help others win too. When we work with others, it's in our best interest—and theirs—to recognize everyone involved.

THE PRINCIPLES OF WIN-WIN

The best way to win in business and in life is to negotiate the victory you aim to achieve. The goal of negotiation is to gain what you value more and to sacrifice what you value less. This can be a long and contentious process, but it doesn't have to be.

When I enter into a negotiation—which is a big component of what I do at JRM each day—I try to approach it with a win-win attitude. I do my best to look at a situation and find a balance that works for both sides, because I believe that the only way an arrangement can work long-term is for all parties to feel they benefit from it. If someone gets the proverbial short end of the stick, the agreement won't last long. Whether I'm negotiating with sponsors, broadcasters, or partners who deliver a positive experience for our fans, I don't expect it to work unless we find a way to meet everyone's objectives.

I operate according to two simple principles designed to offer everyone a win. The first is to focus on the goals that we have in common, and the second is to lay out all the facts and options.

Focus on Common Goals

NASCAR is unique among professional sports because of its sense of family and camaraderie. It's a Southern sport that has become national, and the values for which the South is known permeate the NASCAR culture. Generally speaking, we are "down-home." We hold traditional values, we love the USA, we view family as important, we want to be nice, and we want to have fun.

Our sport—especially on the ownership level—is rooted in legacy families that have been involved for generations. This includes not only the Earnhardts but also the Pettys, the Allisons, the Waltrips, and others. We all go a long way back with each other and, believe it or not, we respect and care about each other. Make no mistake: we compete as hard as we can, but we're not cutthroat about it. I want to win every race, but that wouldn't keep me from congratulating a competing owner on a job well done. People throughout the sport share this attitude of friendly competition, and anytime I enter into a business arrangement or negotiation, I do it in that spirit.

I understand, as the other owners do, that one of our shared goals is to provide a great fan experience, which includes stiff, spirited competition. If one of us continually dominates the others, the experience may be amazing for fans of that particular race team, but not for the entire fan base. Each of us has to champion our own individual teams and interests, but we're wise to keep in mind the bigger picture of everything NASCAR is about.

Most professional sports teams are tied to big cities, and sports fans in those cities root for those teams, unless they have a reason to root for a different team. But NASCAR isn't based on geography. People choose a favorite NASCAR driver or team for all kinds of reasons, but where they live usually isn't one of them.

Because we can't count on a natural, built-in fan base, all forty NASCAR teams have to work together to create a good product every season. This fosters a sense of unity among us and gives us all a single motive—the betterment of all of NASCAR.

In addition to offering a great fan experience, other common goals among NASCAR owners include making our sponsors happy, keeping our sport safe, and raising our profitability.

Whatever your field or industry is, you also have goals in common with the people you work with, whether they are employees, vendors, fans, customers, donors, or supporters. You may also share common goals with your spouse or family, goals related to things you want to accomplish or enjoy together or what you want your lives to look like. Asking yourself what those goals are and learning to articulate them clearly will help get everyone on the same page as you open any kind of negotiation. You must know what you are trying to work toward or you are not likely to make much progress. When you know what is valuable to everyone at the table and commit to working toward that while also protecting your own interests and respecting the interests of other parties appropriately, you are moving toward a deal that works for all.

Put All Fifty-Two Cards on the Table

I'm pretty sure no one ever invented a card game called "Fifty-Two Cards on the Table." It's just a phrase Joe Mattes coined and a metaphor for one of the ways we do business at JRM.

Putting all the cards on the table is something I require of myself but also something I ask of others. It's become somewhat of a mantra for us. It simply means, "I will make no effort to tell you only what you want to hear. I will show my hand. I will tell you what

I bring to the table. I will give it to you straight and tell you every-thing I am at liberty to disclose. I expect you to do the same. If we both operate this way and decide to move forward together, that's great. If not, then we both need to move on."

One of the first memorable statements I heard Joe Mattes say when I started working for him in 1995 was "let facts run the show." What he meant by that is that most business decisions come down to nothing but hard facts. If we can't see all fifty-two cards—meaning that we don't know all the facts—we can't make the best decisions. Effective negotiations require facing facts about ourselves, about our organiza-tions, about our employees, about our customers and vendors, about our decisions, about our limitations, about our potential, about our needs . . . the list goes on. To do our best work, we need to be willing to both speak and listen in the context of candid, facts-based conver-sations. The best way to reach our goals is to seek understanding and to communicate honestly, without game-playing or ulterior motives.

Our sport runs on sponsorships. If we don't have sponsors, we don't have race teams. When I consider a potential partnership with a sponsor, I tell that organization everything I think they need to know about us.

In my first job at Sports Image, I worked closely with several accounts. One of the most valuable lessons I learned was to try to figure out their business models and to listen carefully to what their needs were. I still practice that today. I want to know in no uncer-tain terms what a sponsor needs from us, and I articulate clearly what we need from them. We talk about their business model and about ours. I don't want to offer formulas or cookie-cutter solutions; each sponsor is unique, so I endeavor to work hard and be creative in trying to meet each one's needs.

If a conversation concludes with both parties agreeing that we can and should move forward together, we do. I don't ever want to walk away from an important conversation or negotiation wondering what wasn't said. I want to be sure I've heard everything I needed to hear from them and to be confident that I offered everything they needed to hear from me. That kind of transparency and willingness to be real with our partners has served us well.

At JRM, we apply the fifty-two-cards-on-the-table principle not only to our dealings with sponsors and other outside organizations but also to our in-house communications. I believe explanations are important. To the greatest possible extent, the people who work for us need to know why we do what we do. The better they understand the reasons behind our decisions, the more likely they are to support those decisions.

Even so, as we discussed in the chapter on customizing your communication, it's not wise to share everything with everybody. We must be smart and balanced about what we tell people and how we communicate. For instance, not everyone in an organization can see the big picture, and they're not supposed to. That's why different people hold different levels of authority and responsibility. Though we need to be careful about what we tell whom, whatever we can tell people to help them do their jobs better or make better decisions should be done openly, honestly, respectfully, and concisely.

Negotiating isn't easy. Every relationship we're involved in—business and personal—includes some level of negotiation and compromise. Sometimes, these compromises sort themselves out in the course of normal conversation and planning. For example, everyone in our family wins when L.W. takes a hunting trip. He enjoys it, and the rest of us win because we get one-on-one time with each other and we have a happy husband and father at the end of his trip. But we don't approach this as a negotiation, and no one is seeking to "win," so to speak; we look at it as working out our life together in everyone's best interest. Regardless of the label we put on these types of discussions, they lead to a win. Pursuing our common goals and putting all the cards on the table will take us a long way toward arrangements that make sense for everyone involved and for those affected by our decisions.

There's never been a NASCAR winner that didn't have a plan in place to be first to cross the finish line. In the same way, if you aim for the win and put in the hard work of negotiating what it will take to get there, you, too, might find yourself ringing a bell and celebrating.

ELEVEN

MANAGE YOUR EMOTIONS

Being a woman and a business leader in a man's world can be challenging on several levels but never so much as when the topic of emotional sensitivities comes up. Despite the fact that today there are many outstanding women enjoying unprecedented success in roles historically dominated by men, some still view women as "too emotional" to be effective in leadership positions. This is based on a simplistic assessment of gender differences that says that men are rational and women are emotional. Some stereotypes are indisputable, but there is no hard-and-fast rule that applies to human emotions. To that end, I'm doing my best to disprove the myth that women are too emotional to succeed in business or in roles traditionally held by men. We bring to the table what we want anyone else to bring: vision, passion, responsibility, ability, and strength.

From my perspective, both men and women have emotional components; we simply express them differently. I know my dad was emotional on the racetrack. He was intensely competitive and driven to win—and intensity and drive are emotions. It goes without saying that he was intimidating. That's a quality designed to impact other people emotionally.

I've also witnessed strong displays of emotion among men in our sport outside of the competitive arena. The NASCAR world has had its share of tragedy and loss. I have seen grown men cry over the loss of sons, brothers, and on-track enemies who were off-track friends. No matter how hard they competed against each other, they also loved each other. I mention this to say that I do not necessarily agree with the black-and-white theory that women are emotional and men are not. I've seen many gray areas, and I believe it's more complicated than that.

Human beings are emotional beings, and when we deal with other people, there's always a tendency to respond emotionally. The goal for all of us is to turn our emotions, sensitivities, and intuitive abilities into the assets they are instead of the liabilities they are sometimes perceived to be.

Successful men and women meet that challenge head-on and know how to manage their feelings while dealing with the emotions of others in ways that serve their goals instead of hindering them. The key to winning is to know how to handle emotions appropriately. Anyone who leads from the heart can strike the balance between showing a measure of genuine emotion when appropriate and not letting that emotion become excessive or debilitating.

HANDLING EMOTION EFFECTIVELY

People of either sex who cannot manage their emotions can wreak havoc on the people around them—their families, their friends, and their organizations. In a business setting, leaders who have a lapse in emotional control run the risk of damaging morale, affecting the bottom line, or breaking trust with staff. Every reaction—good or bad—has consequences for all those who report to him or her. The way we manage our emotions has an impact on the overall success of the company.

Emotion comes in all kinds of packages. It can be stress. It can be joy or sadness over a development in our personal lives. It can be anxiety over corporate challenges or fear that the business climate will not be favorable for us. It can be passion for the job we do and the people we get to do it with. Regardless of the source of our emotions, we are responsible for handling them well and not letting them govern our business decisions and interactions.

Managing emotions effectively does not mean shutting them down or suppressing them. We can lead with empathy, passion, and compassion without letting everything that happens cause us to react emotionally. We can learn to *respond* appropriately.

I have not always been able to make decisions without letting my emotions affect them. As a woman who was very emotional in her younger years, reaching this point has been a journey of maturity for me. It has also been essential for me as an executive in a male-dominated sport.

When I first went to work for Joe Mattes, he called me "Fireplug," meaning I had high passion and a short fuse. Joe agrees that I'm not nearly as emotional now as I was when we first worked together. He explained:

Kelley gathers facts better now, and she will sleep on a decision. In the early years, she tended to make quick decisions so she could fix a problem fast and get to the finish line in a situation. She has always had a great ability to assess information quickly, but she asks more questions now. She still moves fast, but she processes things differently now and is willing to take more time to get to the right answer.[1]

Some of my development in terms of handling emotions is a function of age and experience, and some of it is, as Joe says, simply from learning to be less emotional in the way I deal with people and scenarios. Here are some of the lessons that have helped me.

Acknowledge the Emotion—Then Give It Time

Trying to ignore or suppress emotion never works. Taken to an extreme, such efforts can even cause physical problems. Emotions are powerful, and they'll nag a person on the inside until they're acknowledged and handled.

For example, let's say someone in the office does something that reflects negatively on your company and on you. Maybe you have a specific policy against the action, but it happened anyway. I'm not talking about a minor incident; I'm talking about a big, bad, *major* incident that threatens the very organization you pour your life into each day, the one that other employees and families depend on for their livelihood. The fallout will be significant and cleaning it up will take time, energy, and money.

Being angry—even furious—about this situation is understandable, but reacting angrily is not smart. Give yourself time to think and let the raw anger die down. If you need to release it by taking a walk, slamming a racquetball against the walls of a court, staring out the window while you fume, or talking to a therapist, that's okay. What is *not* okay is to spew angry words at the people around you so that the office lights up with gossip about how enraged you are. It's also not okay to go home after a tough day in the office and take your frustrations out on your family.

We all need to be in control when dealing with difficult situations. Remember, we always have options. Stop, think them through, speak in a clear, calm way, and, if necessary, call in a public relations or crisis management team. Formulate a reasonable response and execute it as soon as possible—*after* you have calmed down and thought it through.

Focus on the Facts

We shouldn't pretend our feelings don't exist, but we do need to separate our emotions from other aspects of a situation, look at them objectively, and handle them in a rational way. While I value the role of emotions expressed appropriately, I also understand that consulting emotions instead of examining facts can send a situation into a tailspin.

The environment surrounding any professional sport is competitive, and NASCAR is no exception. We work hard for every win, and we have lots of happy emotion when we celebrate a win. Though I try to keep losses in perspective and do my best to keep emotions steady at JRM, some losses are exceptionally disappointing, especially if we are continually defeated. When that happens, I've noticed that we can easily become overly emotional. I hear people spouting off about why we may lag behind. "Is it the engines?" they ask. "Is it the setup of a particular car? Or is it the chassis? Or is it the driver?" These conversations involve a lot of "What if we did this?" and "What if we did that?"

Instead of asking the what-if questions, we can use data to help us figure out what is wrong. We have dynamometrics spreadsheets, speed charts, test sessions, and even a computer program that over-lays a virtual car with a real car to see how they differ on the track. We have all kinds of factual data at our disposal to point us to the places we need to adjust or improve in most cases. In a sport based on performance, it's easy to get emotional, but we need to remember that we don't have to be so intense about our losses. We can settle down, analyze the data, and use that to help us as we move forward.

In your life and in your job, I would encourage you to contin-ually challenge yourself to identify and articulate the facts relevant to the situation, not the feelings surrounding it. One way to do that is to answer this question for yourself: *How can I talk about this emotional situation in an objective way instead of a subjective one?* That simple exercise will help you take the emotion out and focus on the facts that will take you where you need to go. This is an effective way to communicate when emotions may be running high.

Realize Your Emotions Are Unique

When emotional situations arise, chances are that no one else will feel it exactly as you do. Think about it: If a tight financial situation causes you to fear not being able to meet the next payroll, you'll feel the stress in a unique way because you carry a unique responsibility. People around you may be fearful, too, but they will probably be fearful because they have individual families to support, not because the families of the entire employee base are depending on them.

I see this often in our sport because of my relationship with our drivers. I have been around drivers all of my life, and I learned early that no one feels emotion related to racing like a driver does. When something happens on the racetrack—such as having one driver put a competing driver in a bad spot—everyone rooting for the driver in the bad place feels it. But the driver feels it much more intensely than those who are watching from the pits or on television. In that moment, the driver is the one who has invested more than anyone else, the one who is pouring all of his or her physical and mental resources into the race, and the one whose life is on the line. Of course, the team will be frustrated about that, the owner will be unhappy, and the shop workers will be upset. But the driver's emotions will be affected more than anyone else's.

A similar dynamic takes place in your personal life. For example, if you are a parent, no one feels your child's pain or joy the way you do. No one else has invested what you have invested in that young person. No one else has seen what he or she has been through on the journey to where they are now. No one else can cheer for them, hurt for them, or sympathize with them the way a parent can.

The opposite is also true. When your company achieves a great success, no one will feel the joy quite the way you do because likely no one has invested as much as you have.

Maintain Perspective

When something emotional occurs, it can quickly seem like the most important thing happening. It becomes the topic of conversation in the break room and the buzz that goes around while people are waiting for meetings to begin or riding the elevator together. It can feel like your whole life has become about that one issue. But no matter how high the emotions are, they're not the only important thing that is taking place.

In the office, part of your job as a leader is to know when an emotional situation is affecting morale and to help put it in perspective. The way to do that is not to downplay employees' emotional responses but instead to refocus attention to other aspects of the organization.

If I needed to do this, I'd schedule a company-wide meeting to inform everyone of a recent development with one of our race teams; or I'd host a luncheon to highlight the success of a particular department; or I'd send an email announcing an upcoming promotion or event. The purpose of doing this is to remind everyone on the team that we are bigger than any emotional upheaval and that we need to focus on more than that one situation.

At JRM, we had a situation that reminded me that my perspective is not the same as everyone else's. We needed to add workspace, and a group of us thought we knew exactly how to do that: we would turn our employee workout room into office space.

As soon as the fifteen to twenty people who use the workout room heard about that, they became very upset and passionate about keeping it. They were the ones using it every day, so they didn't want to lose it. More than one hundred people do not use the workout room, though, so to us it was expendable.

When representatives of both groups got together, we each shared our perspectives, and we solicited ideas from those who wanted to keep the workout room about how we could increase workspace while still providing them a way to exercise during the workday.

In my personal life, stress can threaten to send my emotions out of control during especially busy or hectic times, and I have to remember to maintain my perspective. One way I do this is to sit down on Sunday evenings and look at the week in front of me. When I see days on which my family members will be pulled in different directions, I come up with a plan to handle them as best we can. That may mean scheduling home-cooked dinners on some nights but choosing grab-and-go meals on others. It may mean canceling or rescheduling something because I realize there is just too much on the calendar and we need time to catch our breath. I look at what *must* be done and what can wait. I consider my priorities and my values, which include happiness, family togetherness, and quality time with the people I love. Sometimes I need to ask myself, *What's the worst that can happen if don't do this?* If the answer is not life altering, I may let it slide.

Turn the Situation into a Positive, Not a Negative

I have found the old saying "Every cloud has a silver lining" to be true. There's something positive in every negative development that takes place, even if we have to look diligently to find it. In the case of an employee who does something to damage your organization's image, the positives would include a chance to demonstrate *integrity* by owning what happened instead of trying to cover it up or spin it; *humility* by offering a sincere apology if applicable; and *strength* by taking appropriate action. It would also afford the company a chance to restate its values and priorities, putting those front and center in everyone's mind. No one is eager for the chance to demonstrate integrity, humility, and strength in challenging circumstances, but when the situation warrants them, they can become the positive that counteracts a negative situation.

Find Healthy Emotional Outlets

As important as it is to talk to the right people during an emotional situation—people you can trust not to leak, who can help you be objective, and who know how to support, strengthen, and encourage you—it's not the only way to cope. Some people journal while others express themselves through music, art, crafts, or other hobbies. Some take a mental break by watching a movie while others spend a weekend on the lake or at the beach. Others consult a life coach or hire extra help at home or in the office.

All of us can manage emotions by keeping our physical bodies strong and healthy through eating right, getting enough rest, exercising, and staying hydrated. I want to elaborate specifically on the importance of getting enough rest. I am diligent about getting adequate sleep. I could stay up all night handling the many matters I'm responsible for, but sleep is when our bodies repair and rebuild, and it's one of the single most necessary functions that enable our bodies to heal and operate properly. When we deprive ourselves of sleep, we're doing ourselves a disservice.

Taking these steps toward better physical health can be challenging when you have a time-consuming job plus a family. But keeping yourself as strong and healthy as possible will position you to handle stress and emotion effectively.

One of the best things I do to keep my emotions in check is self-talk. I regularly remind myself that not everything has to get done today. I think through my priorities and honestly assess what I can accomplish and what I can't at any given time. I then have frank conversations with others concerning what will and will not get done.

When my mother was diagnosed with a serious illness in 2019, I had to deal with emotions and stress on an unprecedented level.

She worked for JRM, and there were days when I was overwhelmed and irrational about everything that needed to get done while she was away from the office for medical reasons. So I started talking to myself each day, assessing mentally what could wait, what could get done and when, and who could help me, in order to make that difficult circumstance more manageable. This kind of self-talk is powerful.

Another way I manage emotions and stress is to delegate tasks and enlist help from others. I don't have to do everything myself. I'm not going to send someone else to watch my children in a sporting event or support them at a school function, but I can definitely use an online delivery service to pick up groceries.

I also try to stop wondering about what others will think. I can't think, *Well, if I don't get this done, then so-and-so is going to be mad.* I live by the adage "It is what it is." Every situation we face is what it is. We can't change it, but we can work through it.

Set Boundaries When You Work with Family

John Gray reminded us that most women in stressful or emotional situations want to talk about how they feel.[2] During challenging times, however, *everyone* needs someone to talk to—a spouse or trusted friend, a therapist, or a minister. Typically, that person does not need to be a coworker.

The exception to having confidants outside the office is when you are part of a family business or a business that has grown out of a close friendship. My closest relationships in life also happen to be with people who work in our organization—my husband, L.W.; Dale; and, until 2019, my mom, Brenda. There's no way I wouldn't talk to them about something that is highly emotional for me.

They're my support system. But they know and respect the boundaries of our relationships, and I trust them completely to keep our conversations confidential.

In family business environments, every family needs to figure out for themselves how to handle stressful or emotional situations and set their own guidelines for communication. If you're the leader, there will be times you have to say something like this to a family member: "You know we've got this situation going on at work, but right now I need to talk to you about it as my husband [or mom or brother, whatever the case may be], not as an employee of the company."

There will also be times when having family members as part of your business benefits you because they will tell you things others wouldn't. They are around colleagues and may hear about concerns or accomplishments you may not be aware of. Often they can gauge morale better than the person in the CEO's office, especially if they are part of the team rather than leading it.

It's hard to see many positives to the way I grew up, but one that has been beneficial to me is that I learned to keep my work life and my family life separate. Had my dad been totally in control of my career, he probably would have hired me in one of his businesses. The way it worked out, Dale and I didn't work closely with Dad, so neither he nor any other family member served as my direct boss. That distance was a good way to learn how to keep my professional life and my personal life from becoming enmeshed. Anyone involved in a family business must learn how to separate the two. Otherwise, every part of life can get messy, fast.

It's been quite common over the years for me to work with family members. I've learned that when you need to have a difficult conversation with a family member, stick to the facts. Make the conversation as impersonal as possible. For example, instead of saying, "We are writing you up because you are always late. I know that's because you have to feed the babies, but it's still a problem," you could say, "Our employee handbook is pretty specific about tardiness and whenever anyone is late repeatedly, we have to take action." This can help the family member see that what you are doing is not personal but related to the needs of the company.

I have also learned not to gossip or talk with family members about other employees. Even if the family member is in a position to have confidential information that you also know—or should be informed of—that conversation belongs on a professional level, not a personal level. You can always ask yourself, *Would I share this information with other employees who are not family members?* or *Would it be appropriate for someone who is not in my family to share this with me?* when evaluating whether you should share something or let someone else share something with you or not. Certain professional lines shouldn't be crossed.

I've had several experiences in which family members were hurt or offended because I didn't disclose certain things to them before others in the company learned about it. For example, people have said to me, "Why didn't you tell me we had signed this new driver? I can't believe I didn't know that until the press release went out!" I had to learn to say, "It isn't my place to share that with you before it went public because it had nothing to do with your specific role at JRM." Information travels quickly these days, and I believe that being selective in what we share is the only way to manage information effectively.

Setting good boundaries isn't always easy, and people don't always like them. Family members, especially, may test your professional boundaries because they have a different relationship with you from that of other employees. This is exactly why the boundaries are important!

BE YOUR COMPANY'S BIGGEST CHEERLEADER

I realized early in my journey that one advantage to being in touch with your emotions is that you can harness them in ways that enable you to become your company's biggest cheerleader.

When our team experiences a big victory, I can be enthusiastic and even a little goofy. In those moments, no one has ever accused me of being too emotional. I will admit, I also think I can be more of a cheerleader because I'm not in the middle of the specific competitive decisions that determine whether we win or lose. I'm as invested in winning as everyone else is, but because it's not my job to figure out those racing strategies, I don't deal with the pressures involved in winning specific races as much as others do.

When I slide into cheerleader mode, about half of the people around me look at me like I'm crazy. The rest get behind it because they want to be cheerleaders too. They're invested in the win, and they want to celebrate it.

If you've ever watched cheerleaders carry out their roles, you know that when their team is behind, they stay upbeat, almost as though their bright smiles seem to be painted onto their faces. Even if their team is being crushed by an opponent, cheerleaders stay peppy and try to get the fans to rally and support the team. When fans, players, or coaches seem discouraged, cheerleaders keep cheering until the last second goes off the clock. That's just what cheerleaders do. Their jobs are not difficult when their team is winning, but when the team is losing, they have to work extra hard.

From the good cheerleading squads I've seen over the years, I've learned to keep rooting for my team no matter what. JRM has had good years and not-so-good years. Everything hasn't always turned out the way we hoped it would. We haven't always reached the goals we wanted to achieve, even when we did our best. When we face that type of adversity, I do my best to stay positive.

Here's the thing: you can't be both a cheerleader and a Debbie Downer. Well-timed displays of excitement and enthusiasm under the right circumstances serve your organization well; public displays of discouragement or frustration do not. A wise person knows how and when to express the positive emotions and not the negative ones.

Every race weekend across our industry, people experience "the thrill of victory and the agony of defeat."[3] In NASCAR, no one is able to pinpoint exactly why one team wins and the others lose. There are so many factors, and even the most miniscule adjustment can potentially give a team a split-second edge that might make the difference between first place and second. It's a continual process to dig and work for that edge.

For me, a loss on the racetrack is disappointing, but I wouldn't call it *devastating*, because it's not. Earthquakes in Haiti are devastating; wildfires in California are devastating; tragic accidents are devastating. Losing a race is not, and even if we have a particularly painful loss, I have to keep that in perspective.

I would violate my personal standard of professionalism if I were to show up at the office on Monday morning after a disappointing race weekend and stomp my feet or slam doors because I was angry about a loss. It would also be inappropriate for me to mope around and act depressed. The appropriate, professional response is to quickly put a loss into perspective, focus on what our team can learn from it, and get everyone back to work doing what we need to do to win next time.

My job is to keep the team going strong when they are discouraged or disappointed. I get into the same mode cheerleaders do when their teams are down by a large point spread. I must offer the motivation, support, and resources everyone needs—and I have to do that from a place of authenticity or else it won't be effective. Every time we lose a race, I truly believe we can figure out how to win next time, and I use my position as our company's biggest cheerleader to spread that message throughout the organization.

Putting emotions in a place of strength, not weakness, is up to you. My desire is that you will never feel pressure to "turn off" your emotions, but that you will recognize them and handle them appropriately, wisely demonstrating that they are assets instead of liabilities.

TWELVE

BALANCE YOUR WORK WITH YOUR LIFE

In an October 2018 edition of *Forbes*, career coach Ashley Stahl wrote about a woman named Emily, but she could just as easily be named Kelley—and she might even be you.

Emily was consumed by her work. It bled into her personal time—she even took phone calls at the dinner table—and left her feeling like she was missing out on her life. Ashley observed,

> When you want to succeed, it's tempting to put every ounce of yourself into work. But when you do this, you leave very little for other important aspects of your life like family, hobbies, and general personal happiness.
>
> I knew if Emily kept going the way she was, she would burn out, lose productivity at work *and* her connection to her personal life.[1]

I can relate to Emily's story. After I married L.W. at age thirty-eight and had a baby at age thirty-nine, I said to myself, *Something's gotta give.*

Prior to that, I had poured myself into Dale's business and JRM. My two daughters—Karsyn and her younger sister, Kennedy— seemed content with how our life worked, and I didn't realize what we were all missing out on in terms of family time. Adding a mean- ingful relationship with my husband to my life, along with adding a new member to our family, put all of this into perspective.

When L.W. and I married, he wanted (and at times insisted) on having my attention, which was good for us because it kept me accountable. He asked me to put our family first. I struggled at first, but I soon began to see the importance of prioritizing my family. As I started to recognize the difference "family first" made to us, I started saying no to more and more business and outside interests so I could better focus on our family time.

Looking back, I can see that before I had a family, I was a terrible boss. I have always had a strong work ethic, and I demanded a lot from myself and from those who worked for me. Before I had chil- dren, when an employee needed to be away from the office with a sick son or daughter, I thought, *What do you mean you can't come to work because your child is sick? You've got a job to do!* Now that I'm a mother of three, I may be one of the most sympathetic bosses on earth when it comes to children who don't feel well! As is the case with many aspects of leadership, I had to have certain per- sonal experiences in order to develop professional empathy toward others.

You may be familiar with the phrase "Happy wife, happy life." Basically, it means that when a wife is happy, her husband is happy too—and his life is much easier than it would be if she were miserable. The same principle applies in professional settings: happy families, productive employees. When you can model an effective life-work balance for your team, it sets a valuable intangible standard that serves each person in the organization well.

Developing an effective life-work balance was important to me because I never experienced it as a child. In my growing-up years, my dad was great at the "work" part, but not at the "life" part or at any sort of balance between them. For him, everything revolved around racing. I don't remember him ever watching Dale or me in a school play, seeing us off to prom, or attending our graduations. He simply didn't make time in his life for those activities. They may not have mattered to him, but they mattered to us. When I became a parent, I decided to do things differently.

Dale and I had a mom who longed to be with us and to support us in every way but sometimes was unable to do so because she didn't live close to us. Because I grew up yearning for my parents to be deeply involved in my life, I firmly believe that being available and present in the meaningful moments of a child's life—whether that child is eight or eighteen—is extremely important.

As parents, we have only one chance at the significant times in our children's lives. We do not get those moments back. Our children are young only once. They experience being a child only once. They have one shot at the moments of childhood.

Being available to my children and being part of their significant experiences with them will help them grow into well-rounded adults. My presence communicates to them that what they're doing matters and is important. Hopefully that inspires them to put forth the effort needed to do their best in whatever they're trying to accomplish. Most of all, it creates good memories, which I believe are meaningful for all of us, regardless of our age.

Anyone who tries to strike the delicate balance between personal life and professional life faces choices. Some of those choices are difficult because of conflicting schedules or competing interests. Prioritizing family is a decision we won't regret.

A reasonable life-work balance is also important to our professional lives because employees who live balanced lives are more productive than those who don't. Sure, pouring 110 percent of your effort into a job and achieving on a high level as a result is possible, but few people can sustain that kind of intensity on the job for long. Eventually, almost everyone who works that way burns out.

A leader who focuses so intently on the job, pouring everything into it and not making room for balance, tends to be easily irritated and excessively demanding. This results in greater turnover because most employees don't want to live under such high expectations. More than ever, people in the workforce today require a greater life-work balance from their employers. I think we're wise to understand and accommodate that because in the long run it benefits everyone.

FOUR WAYS TO ACHIEVE LIFE-WORK BALANCE

Finding a good life-work balance takes effort and creativity, but it is possible. Everyone, especially women with young children, has to think about their personal and family circumstances to figure out what will be effective. Through the years I've learned some universal principles that I consider life-giving.

Say No When You Need to Say No

Learning how to say no is the most important lesson I've learned about life-work balance. You can't possibly say yes to everything everyone asks you to do. There simply aren't enough hours in the day or days in the week.

Sometimes I'm amazed by the number of requests I receive—everything from being asked to join the board of directors for various businesses or charity organizations; to requests for interviews about NASCAR, Dale, or our company; to one-on-one meetings with clients and employees. But I've learned not to fill my schedule to the point that I feel life is spinning out of control. I have to be able to manage my professional obligations and my personal and family responsibilities without exhausting myself or causing undue stress on the people around me at home and at work.

I know many people—women in particular—who say yes when they need to say no. One reason is that we worry about disappointing people. I understand that. No one wants to disappoint others. But the fact is most people are busy, and they can respect that you're busy too. Family and true friends who see your life up close and personal will certainly understand. If they don't, that's their issue, not yours. All you can do is the best you can do. And when you can do no more, the smartest, kindest thing you can do for yourself is to say no.

I regularly say no to participation on various boards, business networking events, industry dinners and awards ceremonies, and other activities. I also occasionally decline invitations to gatherings with friends or catching up with people I haven't seen for a while. In a situation that hits closer to home, my daughter Karsyn is doing well in her racing career, and I often have to say no to attending her events because it simply isn't physically possible to travel to her races while also being other places I need to be. In fact, I've missed some very exciting wins that I would love to have shared with her, but I can't be two places at once. I go to as many of her races as possible, and she knows I am her biggest cheerleader, but still I would like to do more.

On the other hand, I recently had to miss JRM's season-opening win because two family conflicts—a family member's illness and my son's birthday—fell on the same day as the race. I am a family-first person, and I knew that family needed to come before racing that particular weekend.

Life is filled with competing priorities, and often tension can exist between home and the office. Choosing between them can be difficult, but for me, family wins.

Keep Work at Work and Home at Home Whenever Possible

In a family business, separating work life and personal life can be difficult. L.W. and I face this challenge every day. We often find ourselves discussing work situations when we're not at work—such as when we're driving somewhere or even when we're at home—simply because we catch ourselves thinking about an office issue off-hours. We may think our children aren't listening to us "talk shop" if they're distracted by their phones or watching television. But we quickly find out that they *are* listening, especially when my daughter Kennedy reminds us that we're at home and should stop talking about work.

Not only do L.W. and I work together at JRM, but we also work with my brother and with other family members, including my uncle, my aunt, several cousins, a brother-in-law, and, until recently, my mom. Sometimes the cast of characters at our office feels like the same group of people who would attend a family reunion! That has made keeping work at work and home at home challenging.

There are situations that blur the boundaries between work and home. Several times a week, someone calls me after hours with a work situation that can't wait until the next day, and I must address it. Other times, for schedule reasons, I really do need to have children or the dog at work with me. This is what balancing work and life looks like sometimes. We all have to be flexible. We do the best we can, knowing we won't always do everything perfectly but continuing to strive for what is best for ourselves, our families, and our lives outside the office.

Keeping the various parts of our lives separate is nice but not always possible. Sometimes the best way to keep everyone tended to and to keep everything moving ahead in the most efficient way is to allow a little overlap.

At other times, though, there is no substitute for separating your business life and your personal life completely. L.W. and I do this at least once a year. We take a trip to celebrate our anniversary, and we completely disconnect from work and the demands we face at home, unless there is an extenuating circumstance. For example, when we took our trip in early 2019, each of us had a parent who was dealing with medical issues, so we made ourselves available for daily conversations with them, their spouses, and their caregivers. In those situations, we needed to be involved, and that is why I say to try to keep home and work separate—*whenever possible.*

Phones and email have made certain aspects of communication easier but other aspects harder. For example, we can send a text and bring closure to a situation in a matter of seconds instead of having to schedule a meeting or conference call. But the expectation of quick response and 24/7 availability can result in unwelcome intrusions into our personal lives.

When I get home from work in the evenings, I put my phone on the kitchen counter, out of reach, and I check it only once or twice before bed. I also try not to generate or answer emails outside of work hours. This can be challenging because when I think of something, I want to send a note right away so I don't forget about it!

I tell our staff that they're not expected to answer emails after hours or on weekends unless the message is pertinent to an event or some pressing situation that falls within the confines of their job description. I've even replied to employees after hours or on weekends with "I'm off work. Talk Monday."

For me, weekends are reserved for family unless we are watching a race on television. Part of being in the racing business is that we race on weekends, and I have to be aware of what's happening. If I know Dale is traveling, I hold any work-related emails and texts for him until he returns. I try to extend that same courtesy to others if I'm aware they are away on family or personal business. In the same way, I also try to check with those who I know are experiencing personal problems—whether those struggles are medical, relational, or in some other area of their lives. I want to make sure they know I'm there to support them and that I'm keeping them on my mind and in my prayers.

Make Family Important

Work has a way of making itself important. Almost all day long, we can see a stack of work to do or a list of emails to respond to. We have our phones within arm's reach almost all the time, and people call or text us if they think we won't get back to them quickly enough via email.

Family, on the other hand, doesn't always prioritize itself to you in the same way. The people we love are always there. We see them every morning and every night, and it can be easy to take them for granted. Especially when a work matter is urgent and a family matter can be moved to the next day, our work can appear to be more important than family.

We expect home to be the place we can unwind after a busy day, but too often we take work home with us. We expect our families to love us unconditionally, but if something at work upsets us, we may arrive home angry and unintentionally take out our frustrations on our spouses or children. In situations like this, I have had to learn to stop myself and remember that my children and husband don't necessarily know what kind of day I've had. I need to work hard at not allowing my work-related stress to affect my attitude toward my family. That can be difficult, and it requires mental work, self-talk, self-reflection, and discipline.

Employees, likewise, truly appreciate a work environment that values family. They tend to be more productive when they know they can occasionally leave an hour early without taking paid time off. In our company, they respect the fact that I respect family, and they typically compensate somehow for times they need to be out of the office. I give them flexibility for family matters, and they give me the work I need.

I also understand that family pressure, whether it comes from a spouse, children, or aging parents, can affect job performance. If employees have stressful family situations on their minds, that stress can build up and have a negative impact on their work. I would rather an employee take a little time to deal with a family matter and resolve it than to let it be a distraction at work day after day.

Sending the message that family is important is a priority for me, and I'm committed to being flexible with others where their families are concerned. Will people take advantage of someone who values family the way I do? Yes, they will. I always want to know when people abuse our generous attitude toward family (and interestingly enough, I *do* find out), but I would rather err on the side of giving them what they need than on the side of being too restrictive about family concerns.

Develop Outside Interests

Holding a high-pressure job in addition to being a spouse and a parent leaves little time or energy for anything else. If you have other important relationships with family members or friends, you may have even less time to spend on yourself. But developing hobbies, interests, or other activities that nourish and refresh you is extremely important. It gives your soul room to breathe and keeps your everyday life from becoming completely consumed by the responsibilities and relationships of home and work.

Because of your obligations, you may not currently be able to take up a hobby like golf, because playing eighteen holes takes several hours. But you might be able to take a thirty-minute yoga class at a local gym. Time constraints and responsibilities may prohibit you from going to the beach with your best friends for a week, but perhaps you could go for a weekend. You might not have time to make scrapbooks for each of your children, but you can keep your phone handy to snap photos of moments that are meaningful for them and use an app that will create the scrapbook automatically—or just give them the photos.

Sometimes you will feel that your entire universe is composed of home, the car, and the office, but that's not the way life is supposed to be. There are many ways to expand the scope of your life experiences without compromising your commitment to the people or the job that matter most to you. I encourage you to think about one thing you could really enjoy and look for a way to start doing it today. Chances are, that act of doing something for yourself will give you a needed breath of fresh air and enhance your ability to do a great job at home and at work.

CREATING THE CULTURE OF A LIFE-WORK BALANCE

Years ago, many people intended to stay at whatever company they worked for until they retired. That rarely happens anymore. Today, most people expect to work at several companies over the course of a career, and they plan to change jobs based on what they want out of life.

One way to be the person everyone wants to work for or with is to intentionally create a work environment that respects life-work balance. Of course, as a leader your role is to meet your organization's goals, and that requires having employees who are focused, diligent, and committed to doing their jobs thoroughly and well. But when they can be all of those things and also feel valued as people, not like a cog in a corporate machine, they're more likely to give their best. There are several ways you can create life-work balance for the people on your team.

Offer Competitive Pay and Generous Benefits

Let's face it: most people work for only one reason, which is to earn money to live. Having employees who love their jobs regardless of the compensation is great, but it's rare. Just ask yourself how many of the people who work for you would show up next week if they knew they wouldn't get paid. They're working for a paycheck, just like you are. The better the paycheck is, the more a job seems worth doing. The more a company invests in its workers, the more willing the workers are to invest in the company. If an employee feels the need to have a second job in order to cover each month's bills, that puts even more weight on the "work" side of the scale and less on the "life" side.

One way to let employees know that you respect their lives outside of work is to provide benefits and retirement plans as generous as you can wisely afford. When the people who have worked for me are ready to retire, I want them to feel that JRM treated them right.

Years ago, companies offered health insurance, sick days, vacation days, and some type of retirement program. Today, benefits are much more flexible with stock options, paid time off, mental health days, sabbaticals, postmortem support for the families of deceased employees, and even benefits as specific as days off because of domestic violence. At JRM, we offer what makes sense for us, which is a benefits package that is competitive with other employers in our industry.

Be Creative with PTO

I have tried to make our paid time off (PTO) at JRM as flexible as possible for our employees. We offer them an allotment of PTO that they can use for vacation days, sick days, personal days, or other purposes at their discretion. We also allow employees to donate PTO to fellow employees in difficult or unusual circumstances, such as an extended illness during which the person has exhausted all of his or her paid time off and is still unable to return to work.

JRM employees accrue PTO with each pay period, which means that there may be times they don't have enough PTO yet to cover several days off if they need them. In those cases, they can borrow against future PTO, up to one week, as long as they will eventually earn it. In addition to that, one of the gifts we give at our Christmas parties is extra PTO.

Allow Work-from-Home Options and Flexible Hours

Sometimes there is no substitute for having every member of your team in-house every day. Having them all together creates an important synergy needed to move the company forward, and it often helps the business run more efficiently. But for various reasons, work-from-home options are appealing to many employees.

Some jobs can be done effectively off-site, and some can't. For example, the technicians in our race shop cannot work from home because they have to have their hands on the cars every week, but marketing people can come up with promotions or write copy anywhere.

Technology makes it easier than ever for employees to work remotely. Allowing an employee to work from home for a specified amount of time, such as one day a week or five days a month, is extremely beneficial from a life-work balance standpoint. For a working mother to be able to work at home and get up from the computer just long enough to get laundry done or to be there for repairs or deliveries is a huge help to her. For a dad to be able to offer to coach his child's sports team or lead a scout troop is meaningful to him and to his family, but he can only do it if he knows he can show up for practices, games, or meetings. Working from home can make this possible.

From the perspective of life-work balance, flexible hours are sometimes as important as the chance to work from home. In fact, in an online survey of 6,266 workers, LinkedIn determined that almost half of American workers "would forgo the corner-office job and a high salary to gain more flexibility in their schedules."[2]

For many families, just a little bit of flexibility in the start or stop time at work makes it possible for them to drop off or pick up their children at school. For employees who care for aging parents, being able to work extra hours for a couple of days during a week can allow an opportunity to take a parent to a doctor's visit. These small schedule adjustments allow employees to maintain important responsibilities in their personal lives.

Some of the services people need in order to keep life running smoothly do not have flexible hours, such as school or medical appointments. When I can help my employees get those things done, as long as I know they will also fulfill their work responsibilities, I am glad to do so.

Our office opens at 8:00 a.m. and closes at 5:30 p.m. Within those parameters, people can choose how to work eight hours each day. They can take a thirty-minute lunch break or an hour lunch break during that period of time, and they can arrive at work or leave work as they choose, as long as they complete an eight-hour shift. I want us to allow as much flexibility as possible, while still making sure everyone is working an eight-hour day or a forty-hour week.

But JRM is not composed solely of office employees. We also have people whose jobs focus on competition. Our industry runs on a racing schedule that includes lots of working weekends. Because our business requires race teams to travel on weekends, they typically have one day off during the week. This means they still have a five-day workweek; it's just not Monday through Friday.

Winning at work is important, but so is winning in life. You want to be a great leader in your career, but you also want to be a great spouse, parent, family member, friend, and contributor to your community. Everyone has a list of the things they want to do well and to enjoy. Before we move on to the next chapter, let me ask you a question: What does winning mean to you?

As you think about the answer, you'll find that some aspects of what you are currently doing are necessary for that success and some are not. As you develop a healthy life-work balance, find ways to invest more time and energy in the things that matter most to you and less in those that don't. This sounds simple, I know, but it's a proven way to find a life-work balance that works.

THIRTEEN

LEAD FROM THE HEART

Of all the lessons I've learned over the course of my life and career, one of the most essential is to lead from the heart—that part of me that runs on passion, intuition, and care for other people. The word *heart* has several definitions and is used in various ways. Sometimes it refers to an emotion or to the ability to feel emotions, but I've already written about handling emotions well, and that's not what this chapter is about. Sometimes the word *heart* is associated with softness, sensitivity, or "woman's intuition," but I have known many men, starting with my father and including my brother, who also live and lead from the heart.

The word *intensity* best captures my dad's heart. Dale is intense, too, especially in a racecar, but he also has a gentle quality about him. Everyone who knows him recognizes him as a man of tremendous heart. His style of leadership is more low-key than Dad's was, and he's not as interested in being deeply involved in the business aspects of his career. That's why he hired me! But he's a leader in his own unique way, and he always leads from the heart.

Dale and I have similar hearts. That's one reason we work so well together. We both value integrity and honesty; we both respect others; we both have soft spots for people in need; we're both committed to family; we share a passion for the things that make NASCAR unique; and we're both driven to do all we can to see our JRM teams win races.

A FINE LINE

Leadership is never easy, but sometimes it *feels* easier if we slide into the office through a private entrance, keep the office doors closed, and present ourselves as measured, in control, and somewhat removed from or "above" the situations happening around us. It may seem unnecessary to make this point, but the one prerequisite of leading from the heart means *having* a heart and allowing people to see it.

While some believe that allowing others to see their hearts will cause them to be viewed as "soft," it's more often that people in leadership simply don't think about giving others a window into their hearts. The idea never occurs to them. They may struggle to balance competing priorities involving corporate vision, values, productivity, profitability, and more. They may feel that there's no time left to notice or heed what is happening in their hearts. I want to encourage you to not only sharpen your skills but to pay appropriate attention to the matters of the heart, allowing those around you to know that you have a heart for them.

No doubt there is a fine line to walk. Because of positions and perceptions, it's important to maintain a high level of professionalism and a demeanor that assures people that the organization is strong and stable and that things are under control. Leading from the heart means striking the balance between feeling and showing a measure of genuine emotion when appropriate, while not allowing that emotion to become excessive.

While I was writing this book, the forty-first president of the United States, George H. W. Bush, passed away. The one description of him as a boss and a leader that filled the airwaves was that he was kind. Colleagues and those who had worked for him consistently praised him as a warm, gracious, and extraordinarily kind man. In one television interview, a former staffer recalled that Bush not only knew the names of the White House gardeners, but he also knew their children's names and where they went to school. A man stood in line to pay his respects at the United States Capitol, and when a television reporter asked him why he was willing to wait outside in the cold December air for hours to pass by the former president's casket, he shared a personal story. He had volunteered for more than one of Bush's campaigns. The first time, he met the candidate at an event. The second time, Bush saw him, remembered his name, recalled their first meeting, and gave him a hug.

For days during the week of December 2, 2018, the United States and the world heard stories about a leader with heart, a man who became the leader of the free world and who personally cared about them. Yet no one ever referred to him as "soft." This man, so instrumental in the fall of the Soviet Union and the reunification of a divided Germany, this man who was commander in chief of Operation Desert Storm and a heroic World War II naval aviator, was as strong, dignified, and professional as any leader in recent memory. But when his life on earth was over, he was remembered as much, or more, for his kind and caring heart as for his achievements.

UNDERSTAND THE PEOPLE YOU LEAD

You may be familiar with the television reality show called *Undercover Boss*, in which chief executives disguise themselves as new employees in certain areas of their companies. For example, the show might follow the CEO of a plumbing company pretending to be an apprentice on his first day at the job. That experience would give him a chance to meet a dispatcher, do the dirty work of unclogging a drain or a toilet, make a mistake, and as a result, deal with an unhappy customer and a confrontation with his immediate supervisor.

While he or she is undercover, the CEO realizes that all the people who work in the company are real human beings with real struggles, real hopes, real families, real fears, and real dreams. The point is for the leader to spend time doing what employees actually do each day, to understand the problems and challenges they face, to hear their ideas about ways to make the company better, and, in the end, to do something nice for them that they could not do for themselves.

I can see why some people enjoy the show, but I would encourage leaders not to *need* to go undercover in order to understand their employees' needs, challenges, and victories. Instead, we should take ourselves down from the high altitude of an office or title so we can understand what people do all day, every day.

When I first started working in NASCAR, I tried to learn everything I possibly could about all aspects of the business. I believe that experience has helped me gain credibility. For example, I've answered phones, been an account executive, and managed a call center; I even did my brother's accounting early in my career. I know my way around a race shop. Shoot, I even learned to weld! I can speak the language of drivers, sponsors, crew members, and fans.

I've never driven a racecar at the level on which our drivers do today, but driving was once my greatest passion. Nothing thrilled me more than to put on a fire suit, crawl behind the wheel, and take off at top speed. When I see our JRM drivers get into their cars on race days, I can relate to the way they feel. Granted, the competition is more intense than I ever faced, but I understand the emotion and passion of a driver.

Everyone's journey is different, and not all CEOs or executive vice presidents have actually done the work they oversee. For me, having worked at various levels and in many areas in our sport has been invaluable. Because I haven't always held a leadership role, I remember how I wanted my superiors to feel about me as an employee. I wanted to feel I was part of a team, that what we were doing was worth investing in, and that my contributions were meaningful. That's how I want employees at JRM to feel.

Because of my background, I really don't know how to approach what we do except with a team mentality. In our office, I am the boss—that's a fact. Good things happen to me because I'm the boss, and certain perks go with the job. At the same time, I don't view myself as above anyone else, and I don't want other people to see me that way either. I want them to know I understand what they do and that I truly believe each one of them is an important color in the big picture we're painting together every day. Making us a better unit includes recognizing every individual's talents, skills, and commitment. Our business is not "me" and "them." We're in it together, and I expect everyone to be all in, myself included.

What's most important is that the people we lead know we care about what they face in their jobs and that we want to make their work easier, more efficient, and more fulfilling.

LET THEM SEE YOUR HEART

In CBS's *Blue Bloods*, Abigail Baker is the executive assistant to New York City police commissioner Frank Reagan. One of her duties is to arrange the logistics for his hospital visits to wounded or fallen officers. In one episode, Abigail's husband, a police officer, is shot and critically injured in the line of duty. As is his custom, the commissioner visits Abigail's husband in the hospital as she sits by his side.

Later in the episode, Abigail returns to work while her husband continues to recover, and she tells Commissioner Reagan that she has always been happy to arrange his hospital visits to fallen officers, but until her husband was seriously injured, she never understood how important and meaningful his visits were to officers' families. As his assistant, she knows firsthand his commitment to the individuals of the police force, but as the wife of an injured policeman, she treasures the fact that he cares enough to personally support her during a frightening, unsettling time.

Though she doesn't mention it, Abigail knows the commissioner truly understands what families feel; his own son had been shot and killed in the line of duty. Knowing how much the commissioner cares for her and her husband doesn't make Abigail think he is a softie; it strengthens her already-deep respect and appreciation for him.[1]

At JRM, we hold managers' meetings every week that are intended to focus on results. This includes progress reports from each department and discussions about how to improve efficiency or solve problems. Our human resources manager attends the meeting and updates us on new hires, retirements, or other status changes among employees. If an employee is scheduled to be away from work—whether for a planned surgery or family leave, an unforeseen emergency, or even a dream trip to celebrate a big wedding anniversary—she mentions these situations. She calls them to management's attention, of course, so we can plan appropriately for any extended absence, but also because she knows that caring about our employees is part of our culture. I make a mental note to follow up personally with those employees the next time I see them to ask how they are and to let them know we missed them and are happy to have them back.

I've heard countless stories from my dad's former employees that recount the way he knew their names, their families, and what was going on in their lives. This was important to them, and it's important to those who work at JRM too.

We also offer our employees a nonmandatory weekly lunchtime Bible study that gives those who attend an opportunity to mention prayer requests. This provides another chance for me to know what's going on with the people who make our business run. When I hear a request, I try to remember to ask about it the next week. Saying, "Hey, Sue, how did your son do on that big math test?" literally takes only a couple of seconds, but it keeps me connected and shows employees that they have a leader who genuinely cares about them as people, not just as parts of our business machine. I've also shared my own prayer requests and stories, showing those around me my heart and helping them see that my everyday life often resembles their own.

Leading from the heart takes time and effort, but it sends a strong, important message throughout an organization. It tells the people you work with that you're a part of their team. You may be the vision-caster for the organization, but you also *share* that vision and are doing your part to make it a reality. Allowing people to see your heart takes pride out of the equation and communicates that you value your employees—and when people feel valued, they more readily invest in what the organization is trying to achieve. When they see heart exhibited, they will put more of their own hearts into their work.

DO GOOD ON PURPOSE

One of the most important lessons I learned from my dad was to make a point of doing good to others. He often gave his time and abilities to the Make-A-Wish Foundation, among other charitable organizations. In 2007, Dale and I started the Dale Jr. Foundation as a way to focus on a mission and strategize our giving.

Dale is the president of the foundation; I'm the vice president and a board member, and I have hands-on time running the operation. I really enjoy what we do because it allows us to give back to our community and beyond.

I've also served on the board of our local Humane Society, and I'm a board member of Children's Hope Alliance in Barium Springs, North Carolina. I've given my time to initiatives as simple as Dr. Seuss Reading Days at local elementary schools, to a variety of endeavors that are more challenging for me—such as speaking engagements at charitable luncheons—because I find speaking in front of large groups terrifying.

Our dad modeled the importance of helping people, and we try to help others in the most strategic, beneficial ways we can. I know that Dale and I had a leg up in life because of who our father was. That has blessed us in many ways, and we try to give to people who don't have that kind of advantage.

Dale has always had a soft heart for underdogs and people who face difficulties or challenges. He has always cheered for backmarker teams (long shots) and independents, rooting for the ones with less fan support. He says he didn't have to get a foot in the door in racing because Dad's name did that for him. He is quick to acknowledge that all he needs to do is to do good with what he has. The work of the foundation is dear to his heart, and when he talks about it, he says, "To me nothing is more rewarding than to see people's lives take a turn for the better and know you might have had something to do with it."[2]

The focus of the Dale Jr. Foundation is on underprivileged individuals, with an emphasis on youth. Our mission statement summarizes our objective—to give people the resources they need to improve their confidence and education and to have the opportunity to achieve extraordinary goals. The foundation focuses on five areas of giving that are important to us: empowerment, education, wellness, hunger, and hope.

Empowerment

The foundation supports many organizations that provide safe homes for children who come from traumatic backgrounds of abuse or neglect. We partner with these groups to help these children heal from their hurt and to give them a fresh start in life. We help meet their needs for resources to overcome their adversities and regain their sense of self-confidence.

Education

Research shows that children who grow up with strong, positive values are happier and do better in school than those who don't. We invest in education by providing grants for technology, reading incentives, and helping teachers with out-of-pocket expenses. We believe a strong education system is vital to the success of our community.

Wellness

Children need to be physically healthy in order to reach their full potential, so we support organizations that provide child-friendly health services. These organizations are not limited to providing medical services; they offer all forms of holistic care.

Hunger

Nutritious food is an essential building block of a child's physical, social, and educational development. Unfortunately, more than twenty million children face food insecurities each week. We partner with many different organizations that provide nourishment through healthy foods to children who might otherwise go hungry.

Hope

We feel that creating some type of connection with children, no matter how small it may be, is the greatest way to provide them with a sense of normalcy and give them hope for the future. This connection can be the positive experience they need to overcome their obstacles.

We try to be creative in our fund-raising efforts for the Dale Jr. Foundation, and one way we do that is to make the most of what we have. For example, we host an eBay auction in which we auction off autographs, memorabilia, and merchandise such as die-cast cars and racing gear worn by our drivers. We also sell chances to "Win Dale Jr.'s Ride," an opportunity for people to purchase raffle tickets for twenty-five dollars each to win Dale's personal Corvette. We do this each year from March 1 through August 31, and it typically raises more than $250,000 for the foundation.

We also host a special event fund-raiser called Driven to Give, which is the foundation's annual dinner and auction with approximately 350 guests in attendance. We have some really great items available for bidding, and we invite a comedian to cap off the night by helping everyone laugh and have a good time. At this event, we spotlight some of our partner charities and some of the children we work with to show people firsthand how we're helping others.

It's important to me that our charitable efforts not stop with us, but that we also help propel the missions of others. Because of our name recognition, Dale and I are able to raise awareness for nonprofit organizations that may not be able to generate interest on their own; this helps them gain donors. We do this for a variety of local and national charities who partner with us.

People don't need fame or celebrity status to have a heart for others and to do good. Anyone can do good, and that starts with simply helping others. It may not involve giving significant time or money to an established charity; it could be as easy as donating to an individual in need, supporting a friend's fund-raiser on social media, sending a bouquet of flowers to brighten someone's day, being kind and thoughtful, or offering someone a smile. There are many ways to do good in this world. What's important is not how much you give or where you give it but that you allow the needs of others to touch your heart and then do what you can to help them.

— PART THREE —

WHAT I WISH I'D KNOWN

Helping people be happy people is part of my purpose in life. If I could, I would sit with you and talk about your future. I would share with you some wisdom I've gained along the way—some things I wish I had known when I was just starting out.

As you look toward your own future, I hope the insights on the following pages will help you find your path to a rewarding career and a successful, purposeful life. While these chapters are geared toward young adults or people who are just establishing their professional lives, I encourage you to keep reading even if you've got some experience behind you, because we can always learn from the experience of others and decide to make different choices that bring us closer to our goals.

FOURTEEN

PREPARING FOR YOUR RACE

You have read in this book a little about how JRM prepares cars to race. We take them through a careful, detailed process designed to precisely accommodate the driver and the track, and to position the car to win.

I've noticed several parallels between preparing a car to race to victory and preparing for a successful life. For example, just as we wouldn't choose a random car from our shop and take only a quick look at it before sending it off to race, you would not want to head into your future without careful thinking and planning. And just as we make certain decisions about tires and struts, you will need to make choices that will position and carry you toward your personal and professional goals.

I've divided our discussion into three categories—*priorities, passion,* and *people.* I really wish I had understood these better as a young person, because the earlier you can make these decisions the better off you will be. They are absolutely a part of any conversation

I have today with teenagers or young adults who want to know how to thrive on and off the job.

ESTABLISH YOUR PRIORITIES

To establish your priorities, let the people and things that matter most to you determine everything else. Now is the time to think about the things you truly value and to realize that the only way to keep them in the forefront of your life is to make decisions that strengthen your commitment to them instead of weaken it. Stephen Covey, in his *The Seven Habits of Highly Effective People*, wrote, "The key is not to prioritize what's on your schedule, but to schedule your priorities."[1]

I've shared that family is a priority for me. My job is a priority, too, but when I'm forced to choose between the two, family comes first most of the time. In an organized, disciplined, well-balanced life, you can give a good amount of attention to more than one priority. But it's still a good idea to keep in mind the order of your priorities, because there will be times when circumstances force you to choose the one that truly is most meaningful to you.

Your priorities may shift and evolve over time, and that's part of growing as a person. Right now, you may think professional success is more important than anything else, and that's great; one of the keys to a rewarding career is to make it important to you. But if you fall in love and want to marry and start a family with someone, you may change your mind and need to choose family over work in certain ways. This is true for both men and women. Women are often primary caregivers for children, but having a family requires adjustments from men too.

In addition, as your family members begin to age, you may want to maintain your career while also making yourself available to care for them at times, and that will require an adjustment. When you no longer have children or parents who need significant amounts of your time and attention, you can tweak your priorities. And when you reach retirement age and beyond, your priorities may change again.

What's most important is to figure out what matters to you and to pursue those things. There will be seasons when you can tend to only the most valuable people or the most urgent situations in your life, when you feel your top priority takes all of your time and energy. These seasons will pass. Although your priorities may change throughout your life, determining what is important to you at every stage will help you stay focused and make the best decisions you can make.

The late pastor and author Myles Munroe said, "At any point in our lives, we are the sum total of all the decisions we have made, the people we have met, and the facts we have learned."[2] When you think about the fact that your life equals your decisions, relationships, and education—plus your priorities—you realize how critically important priorities are.

MERGE YOUR SKILLS AND YOUR PASSION

Maybe you are one of those people who has known since kindergarten exactly what you wanted to be when you grow up. But maybe you're not; maybe you're still trying to figure it out. Here's my best insight on that: there's a difference between skills and passions.

Your skills are the things you can do, even if you don't particularly enjoy them. Your passions are the things you can't wait to do, and you would rather do them than anything else. *Know the difference between your skills and your passions*, then follow your greatest passion and use your skills to support it. You may have to learn and develop the skills you will need, as I did by getting a business degree, but that's part of building a career you can enjoy.

One of my passions is racing. That's understandable, given my history. Another passion for me is the Earnhardt family legacy. I am diligent and determined to uphold that legacy and our good name throughout our sport and in the world. My dad was as passionate a competitor as our industry has seen, but he didn't just love winning—he loved *racing*. In addition, he also had common sense and a great big heart. Out of those passions, he spoke up for what he believed was right, he influenced off-track issues in NASCAR, and he used his position and resources to help others. Dale and I both inherited his passionate streak, though we demonstrate it in different ways.

I'm passionate about helping people become happy people, but that's not the only thing that drives me, and I'm not looking for a job as Chief Happiness Officer anywhere. I have to express that fervent desire in the context of what people would call "a real job." For me, that job is a leadership role at JRM. That position allows me to do everything I'm passionate about, and it also requires the business skills I've developed over the years. I can't just host a beer toast and cheer for our teams on race weekends; I must also manage budgets and schedules, oversee a team of managers, negotiate contracts, and perform other functions that keep our business running. I can't say I am passionate about reading the fine print of a legal document, but it is a skill I have that supports my passion for being involved in the business aspects of NASCAR.

You may face a tremendous amount of pressure concerning your education and career choice, especially if you're a young person just starting out. You may be feeling stress to choose a certain path because of the money you could make or because of the prestige it would offer. But if you know you would be miserable in that field, I encourage you to think carefully and to talk with people you trust and respect before you commit to it.

If you pursue a college degree, you'll have many options when you choose classes and declare a major. While some people major in a certain subject and then work in an entirely different field, a degree often helps chart a career path. Anyone who has been through college and tried to find a job will tell you that certain degrees are more marketable than others.

Employers understand that some degree programs give you foundational skills you will need in order to develop in their organizations, while others will not prepare you as well. For example, I could have completed the criminal justice major I started in college, but I would have had a much steeper learning curve to gain the business knowledge I needed for my executive position in NASCAR. It wouldn't have been impossible, but I would've lost time and perhaps opportunities. I don't want that to happen to you.

My daughter Karsyn, interestingly, also went to college thinking she would major in criminal justice because she wanted to be an investigator. She discovered that she couldn't be an investigator without first working as a police officer, which she doesn't want to do. Now, she's focusing on her core subjects and rethinking her major. College is the time to do this. People often find work in fields in which they don't have degrees, but there are benefits to choosing a major that will best prepare you for the job you would like.

A business degree was an excellent choice for me; I didn't know exactly what I wanted to do, and it offered me a chance to learn basics that would apply to a variety of professions. My business degree has a concentration in production and operations management, which turned out to be ideal. Other concentrations, such as marketing or accounting, are also available. I still think majoring in business—or at least taking a few basic business courses—is a smart decision. For people in the humanities or liberal arts settings, a degree in English is versatile and provides a solid foundation for further study or for employment in many fields.

Ultimately, only you can decide how you want to prepare for your future. You definitely need to be able to support yourself financially, but I feel that what's most important is to not allow the pressure the world puts on you to pull you into a decision that goes against your heart. This can be difficult when you're young and you feel the need to prove yourself. I encourage you not to let anyone lead you away from the passions of your heart for anything that is not valuable to you. Stay true to yourself, follow your heart, know your passions, and use your skills to support them.

MAXIMIZE THE POWER OF OTHER PEOPLE

Anyone who has been successful in business has had help. Even people who proclaim to be "self-made" have benefitted from others—even if only by reading books or articles—somewhere along the way. Just as fuel powers a racecar and moves it toward victory, the people you meet can form an important network to send you toward success. But you'll have to be intentional about it, and it's never too early (or late!) to start.

As far back as I can remember, I was aware of what people around me did to make a living. The majority of those people were involved in racing, but I also knew people who taught school, rang up groceries, fought fires, fixed plumbing, farmed, or worked as doctors, nurses, bank tellers, or photographers. I'm sure you can also remember being very young and observing different types of people doing different jobs. When we are very young, it is not uncommon to want to do the jobs the adults we admire are doing.

Life has a way of eliminating certain career options. Maybe we lose interest in something we once wanted to do, or we realize that we don't have the aptitude for it and decide to pursue something that comes more naturally to us. Or maybe we don't want to take the necessary steps, as was the case when Karsyn wanted to be an investigator.

Even though you can't work in every field that interests you, the fact that you find a given career appealing is a reason to investigate. When a particular occupation catches your attention, don't hesitate to talk to people involved in it. You can start building a network during childhood, at least unofficially. Plus, plenty of people change careers over the course of their working lives. You never know when you might choose one field over another for a time and then later have a chance to pursue your original plan.

I was born into a network because the Earnhardt name creates an instant connection in and beyond our sport. But I realize that not everyone has such an advantage. You can start networking by simply being around people who work in your field of interest and striking up a conversation with them. If someone were to ask me how to get started in NASCAR, I would say to hang around a racetrack. Spend time in the pit, if possible, or in a garage. Learn everything you can learn about racing so you can ask smart questions and speak intelligently about the industry. Then just start talking to people.

At first, you may speak to people casually, but there will come a time when you need to be more intentional. When possible and appropriate, attend important events in the industry. Contact people in a professional way, such as asking for a few moments of their time so they can provide further insight and suggest ways for you to continue moving toward your goal. Ask them what they like and dislike about their jobs and find out what they wish they had done differently on their paths to success. Have them talk about their greatest accomplishments and gather insight on what they do and why they do it. Be creative and ready to meet and talk to people who can help you. You never know when you might be in the right place at just the right time.

About every other month, I receive a note from a young racecar driver in Pennsylvania. He has been sending me messages on a regular basis for several years because he so strongly wants a chance to drive our cars. He is persistent but not annoying—and that's what it takes. Being able to persevere and keep your name in front of people while still being respectful in your quest for opportunities will serve you well.

CULTIVATE A RELATIONSHIP WITH A MENTOR

Having the right mentors can help you in every area of your life, not just in your professional development. Someone who excels in his or her career can offer you professional guidance and advice. Someone who does an exceptional job balancing personal commitments with work responsibilities can be a great resource for life coaching. If you are a young woman and you choose the path of love and marriage, someone whose abilities you admire as a wife and mother can help. As a young man, someone you admire as a husband and father could be your mentor.

My point is this: before you ask someone to mentor you, know what areas of your life you would like to be mentored in, and ask people who are experts in those fields.

The title of an article in *Forbes* offers great advice to anyone seeking a mentor. It says, in part, "First, Don't Ever Ask a Stranger."[3] You may find your mentor in a schoolteacher or college professor, a friend of your parents, or a neighbor. He or she may be someone you admire who is active in the field you want to pursue. Just make sure you have some sort of relationship with that person, because you will want to know that you can respect and trust him or her.

If you're a young person just starting out, there are many experiences you have not yet had and many lessons you have not yet learned. Having a mentor is important because that person has already walked where you want to go and can help you navigate your path. But working with a mentor can be beneficial to anyone, no matter what stage of life you're in, because we can always learn from people who have achieved the same goals we want for ourselves.

As you gain skills and experience in your chosen profession and your personal life, you may have increased opportunities to mentor others, just as people mentored you. I can tell you from experience that being a great mentor to a young person has as many rewards as having a great mentor when you are young. Learn all you can from your mentor, and when someone chooses you to mentor them, pass it along.

Setting your priorities, combining your passions and your skills, maximizing the power of other people, and developing relationships with good mentors will serve you well in the future and lay a firm foundation for you in and out of the office.

FIFTEEN

GETTING, KEEPING, AND GROWING IN A JOB YOU LOVE

From an early age, many of us hear about the importance of getting an education and choosing a career. We know we're expected to get a job, but we're not always taught how to be good employees. Being able to land a job you love is important, but being able to keep that position, grow into greater responsibility, and secure the leadership role of which you are capable is important too. Whether you're entering the working world for the first time, returning after a long absence, or changing industries, these tips will equip you to go to the front of the field.

GET INVOLVED EARLY

Once you've determined an area of passion or interest for your career, be intentional about learning about it. That could mean joining a school group, volunteering, completing an internship, seeking employment in the industry (even if it's not your dream job), or attending conferences and events related to the field that interests you. You can start doing this as early as middle school or high school, but the closer you get to needing to find full-time employment, the more important it becomes.

Gaining exposure to your area of interest will give you an up-close view of how it works and firsthand opportunities to see if it really is everything you hoped it would be. You'll have the chance to figure out what you love about it and explore what you may not like. As you spend time learning the industry, you may decide you would like to focus on one particular aspect of it, or you may decide it isn't really what you want to do after all. If you can learn these lessons early, you'll be able to move more quickly into something that does appeal to you.

Getting involved also counts as experience on your résumé, and experience is very valuable to employers as you enter the workforce. The more of these opportunities you have on your résumé, the better. Your experience doesn't have to be a paid position; it simply needs to expose you to your area of interest and position you for the next step.

Karsyn has recently decided she may want to attend cosmetology school, which came as somewhat of a surprise to me. I know, though, that if she is serious, she needs to learn more. I've encouraged her to talk to our friends who are hairdressers and to ask specific questions about the profession so she can find out what they like and don't like about it and how they've built a client base. I've also told her to ask if it pays the bills and to investigate other practical aspects of the job. If she still wants to pursue cosmetology, I'll encourage her to seek additional information as she grows older and begin to get experience that will help her.

These days, no career advice would be complete without mentioning internships, which are more important than ever. Each summer at JRM, we have interns in the office and in our engineering department. Many of these interns have become full-time employees for us, and I know this to be true for other organizations in our industry as well.

I see several benefits to internships. For example, they offer an inside look into a company or organization, offering interns to observe the entity as a whole and evaluate what they like and don't like about it. They also serve as good reality checks, because people who have not yet worked in certain places often have misconceptions about what it would be like. For example, a young person may think interior design work would be fun because designers work with colors and fabrics and furniture placement. An internship will reveal that designers also deal with the hassles of colors that don't work as well as they thought, late deliveries, furniture damaged in shipping, as well as the business aspects of design, such as billing and paying taxes. By the time the internship is complete, the intern will have a more holistic view of what he or she wants to do and can make an informed decision about whether to move forward. In addition, internships offer opportunities to network and build relationships that can help develop and advance a career for years to come.

PRACTICE PROFESSIONALISM

I don't know of a school that teaches a course on professionalism, but it's important as you seek employment, compete for promotions, or take advantage of opportunities to advance in your career. You may not have been exposed to many settings that require a professional attitude or professional behavior, but most likely, the people in positions to hire you and help you move forward have worked in a professional environment for a long time. They'll expect professionalism from you, and you would be wise to demonstrate it.

I've been involved in hiring and promoting people for years. Based on my experience, here is a to-do list that may be helpful to you.

1. Honor Positions of Authority and Observe Chains of Command

While I was writing this book, a young person I was aware of through an acquaintance, but did not know personally, emailed me about an internship at JRM. The internship was not in the executive office, so I directed her to the manager of the department in which she wanted to work. After he interviewed her, he became involved in a time-sensitive project that was very important to our company. I understood completely why he was unable to respond to her immediately.

Instead of contacting him to follow up, the candidate emailed me personally, and as you'll see in a few paragraphs, the message was quite rude. The professional way to handle this situation would have been to respect the fact that I had delegated her potential internship to one of our managers and to have honored our chain of command. If she didn't want to email the man with whom she interviewed, she should have emailed human resources, not me.

2. Communicate with Maturity and Respect

I am surprised that I feel the need to say this, but an email to your colleagues or to your boss is not a text message to your friend group. Technically, both are communications, but different audiences require different tones. To communicate in a professional manner, keep the following in mind.

- **Don't use emojis or abbreviations.** The use of "2" for *to*, "4" for *for*, "u" for *you*, or "idk" for *I don't know* are not appropriate; neither are emoji responses such as crying-laughing faces or thumbs-ups.

- **Use proper spelling, grammar, and punctuation.** A misspelled word indicates a lack of effort to get it right. I am continually amazed and annoyed when people spell my name "Kelly" in emails instead of "Kelley." It's on my signature line! Misplaced punctuation can significantly change the tone or meaning of a message. Such mistakes in writing may indicate a lack of attention to detail in other areas of work as well, so pay as much attention to your written communication as you do to other aspects of your job.

- **Acknowledge receipt of a message, especially if you are not able to respond thoroughly immediately.** Sometimes people don't respond to emails or messages because they don't have the information needed or they don't know how to respond. When this happens, it's best not to leave the other person wondering if you received the message. A simple email saying "I just want to let you know I received your message and I am working on getting the answer you need" or "Thank you for your email about [subject]. I did receive it, and I will get back to you by the end of the week" will suffice. The message should be at least one sentence, even if it's brief. The response "k" is highly unprofessional in a business setting.

If you are away from the office for several days or longer, an automatic out-of-office reply allows an email sender to know the message is in your in-box and to expect a reply after you return to work.

- **Respect boundaries.** You may not hesitate to call, text, or email a friend at 10:00 p.m. or on a Sunday afternoon, but that would not be respectful in many work settings. Unless a true crisis arises, resist the temptation to call or text colleagues or superiors outside of business hours.

- **Understand that it's not always what you say—it's how you say it.** An employer or potential employer is not someone you hang out with, and they shouldn't be treated as such. The internship candidate I mentioned earlier wrote in her email: "Because I have not heard from JRM, it appears there are no opportunities for me there." She expressed no appreciation for the fact that I had arranged the interview for her, nor did she word her message graciously. When someone makes an effort to help you, it's not appropriate to be rude or snarky. Even if you're unhappy with the outcome, find a way to word your communication with kindness and respect. (The sad part of the story of this candidate is that the manager had not decided *not* to give her an internship; he was simply behind in communicating with her for a legitimate reason. She might have gotten the position, but after her email, the manager took her name out of consideration.)

3. Manage Time and Resources Carefully

Going from a college environment, in which you may have scheduled only afternoon classes or not had classes on certain days, to a work setting is an adjustment. You may not be accustomed to allowing for rush hour traffic in order to arrive at work on time, and you may not be used to having only thirty minutes for lunch. You may also find the pace of a work environment to be more intense, requiring you to learn to manage your time in new ways. People who are not on time to interviews, to work, or to meetings rarely rise above their entry-level positions, and in many organizations, chronic lateness is grounds for termination.

Having a job will also give you access to resources you may not have had before, everything from office supplies to company-issued phones, laptops, tablets, or even a car. All companies have policies about the use of company-issued equipment. Those resources are for you to use, but they are not your possessions. "Borrowing" a stack of legal pads or a box of pens for personal use is not okay, even if you return them. Be aware of the limitations your organization puts on resources they allow you to use, and be diligent to observe them.

4. Appreciate and Learn from Fellow Employees

When you're excited about a new job, you may be tempted to suggest new and different ways for your colleagues to do their work. You may also be tempted to disregard sound advice that a well-meaning colleague may offer you if it conflicts with what you learned in school.

As a new employee, you should value the experience of the people who have been there longer than you. You may think your new ideas are great (and maybe they are), but many people with longevity in their positions have had time to figure out, through trial and error, what enables them to be most productive. Observe them, ask them questions, appreciate them, and learn from them.

5. Observe Discretion and Obey Confidentiality Requirements

The sharing of interesting or important pieces of information is part of many jobs. As an employee, you'll learn things about your company, its people, and its plans that are considered privileged. In many cases, you'll be required to keep that information confidential. This means not talking about it—or even hinting about it—with family members or friends. Do not discuss it on your phone in a public setting. Keep in mind that there can be serious consequences for breaking confidentiality.

You may also become aware of issues that aren't confidential but do require discretion. For example, in an open concept or cubicle setting, no one's conversations are private. Even when people whisper, others can hear. You may become aware of family problems, financial struggles, or medical situations that are personal. While you're not required to stay quiet about such matters, it's respectful and discreet to do so.

Honoring confidentiality and practicing discretion are marks of strong character. The best leaders are people of character, and if you want to advance to a position of leadership and retain it, you are wise to respect the privacy of company business and the privacy of the people around you.

DEVELOP A STRONG WORK ETHIC

Everything of value in life takes work—usually good, hard, old-fashioned work. Despite the popular idea that certain people are entitled to certain things for certain reasons, the truth is that nothing worthwhile comes easy.

When a potential employer evaluates you as a candidate for a job, you want that person to know you are willing and able to work and that you expect to do your part to contribute to the organization's success. No matter how good your grades were in school or how much potential you think you have, people are not likely to hire you if they don't think you will be a good worker. This is one reason internships and volunteer jobs are valuable: if you distinguish yourself as a person who works hard when you're not getting paid, employers have reason to believe you will work hard when you *are* getting paid.

Several of the managers in our race shop started as entry-level employees; now they're making more money and carrying more responsibility because they proved themselves to be diligent, dedicated workers. They may have been capable of doing more than we originally hired them to do, but we needed to see that. Once we knew we could count on them to do what we needed them to do, we rewarded them.

You may not get the job you really want when you first go to work, but if you will be responsible, be dependable, and put in the hours necessary to do a good job, opportunities for growth will come. No one wants a coworker who doesn't carry his or her share of the load, but everyone appreciates working with a person who is diligent and gets the job done.

My daughter Karsyn once worked for JRM's production company. She ran errands, did grunt work on production days, and carried out whatever task she was asked to do. She often complained that she felt she was doing petty work, but I told her, "That's how you start. You have to be good at that kind of work and show people you're dedicated and reliable to be able to climb the ladder to the next step. Doing those jobs without complaining, doing them in a timely manner, and doing them well shows your boss that you are deserving of more responsibility."

When people have to learn to work later in life, they often struggle. The earlier you realize that very little will be handed to you and that you will have to work hard to earn a living, a promotion, or the lifestyle you desire, the better off you will be.

GAIN A HEALTHY PERSPECTIVE ON RESPONSIBILITY

I've always had a highly developed sense of responsibility. In many settings, being super-responsible is good. It's generally considered a positive trait. Sometimes people with strong leadership qualities are this way because they are smart, capable, and have a high capacity to manage multiple responsibilities. They do it because they *can*. But being a leader in business while also juggling a busy life outside the office requires a healthy, balanced perspective on responsibility and the realization that although some things truly are your responsibility, others aren't. An effective leader knows how to fulfill the responsibilities that are appropriate for her, while wisely delegating the ones others need to carry.

For many years, one way I demonstrated my strong sense of responsibility was to try to protect the people around me, especially Dale. Whenever I could, I did my best not to let anything bad happen to him. If I could take punishment for him or otherwise spare him the consequences of his actions, I did. After all, my role in our family was to be the fixer, the doer, and the one who figured everything out. I felt my responsibility for myself and for Dale was helping him. I truly believed my well-intentioned actions were best for him at the time, but I came to realize later that maybe they weren't.

I didn't understand the difference between real responsibility and false responsibility. False responsibility is simply taking responsibility for people or situations that aren't yours. I had to learn the hard way that taking on false responsibility can be exhausting. More seriously, it can rob others of opportunities to mature.

Both at work and in other areas of life, it is important not to carry other people's baggage. People have to make choices every day; the best course of action for us is to let them make those choices and allow them to live with the consequences so they can learn and grow. This doesn't mean refusing to give advice or appropriate help if they ask for it. It simply means not intervening excessively in order to keep them from struggling in some way, because the right struggles become stepping-stones for success. Take responsibility for what is yours—and don't for what is not. In a business setting, everyone is an adult and each person is responsible for his or her choices.

I hope the suggestions I've mentioned are helpful to you. If you will apply them, along with other valuable lessons you learn as you move toward your future, you'll position yourself to lead with integrity and compassion.

SIXTEEN

BE YOUR BEST SELF

As much as I appreciate my business degree and my work experience, much of my success doesn't have its origins in a diploma or a job description. The success I've experienced is rooted in my experiences as a daughter, a sister, a student willing to learn from other people, and a woman who finally found healing and inner peace. Only then could I rev the engine of my mind behind a desk all day long and make a significant impact. Until my childhood wounds were healed, I made adult decisions rooted in a young person's pain. I had to learn how to become healthy in my mind and soul before I could move on. Some of those lessons I learned the hard way.

Some people are surprised when I say I've learned things the hard way. They think that because of who my father was, my life has been charmed. But it hasn't. Just like you, I've known struggles and heartache, loneliness and unfulfilled longing. I've made mistakes and suffered failure. I've made bad decisions that have caused pain for me and for others.

I've also been blessed to take a life-changing journey of healing and wholeness. It has been a sometimes agonizing, always emotional, exhausting yet rewarding adventure of growing into the person I was meant to be. That journey has been critical in my success, and I couldn't write about winning in business and in life without having taken it.

For years, I had the experience and intelligence to lead a large company; I learned quickly how to run a successful racing organization. But I needed personal transformation in order to lead effectively. That transformation has empowered me to run the business in an entirely different way from how I did previously and to lead people not only with my head but also with my heart. What has helped me in business and in life is not so much what has happened *around* me—the up-close exposure to the ins and outs of the racing world, my pedigree, and my connections or work history—as what has happened *inside* of me.

PAY ATTENTION TO WHAT'S GOING ON IN YOUR HEART

No matter what strengths or skills we bring to our jobs, our work can quickly feel empty and pointless if we can't pour our hearts into it. When we bring our hearts to our work and to our colleagues, our careers become points of passion and purpose. Once I paid attention to my heart and worked to heal to it, I gained a greater awareness of the importance of living with a sense of meaning and purpose and connecting with people in my life.

When you're busy and stressed, as often happens when you seek to win at work and outside it, it's easy to ignore your heart—your innermost thoughts and feelings, past and present. Trust me—these affect you more than you may realize.

I needed to pay attention to my heart long before I actually did it. It wasn't until I saw my daughter Kennedy struggling with issues related to the divorce between her dad and me that I made my heart a priority. I felt she needed therapy, and before long, I realized I needed therapy too!

During my first visit with my therapist, I said, "I feel weird being here because nothing that I would consider really bad has ever happened to me. I wasn't sexually abused. No one ever hit me. I have just struggled for so long because I never felt loved. I never felt worthy, and I never felt that I mattered."

I share this because I know that many people have been through situations or relationships that were not good for their hearts. If that's you, I hope my story will encourage you to not be afraid to seek help. You can be the person you long to be and do the things you long to do. If something in your heart is holding you back, you can deal with it and move forward with confidence toward a life of love, joy, peace, passion, and purpose.

In my early days of therapy, I cried about everything. The therapist was good about stopping me when the tears began to flow and asking me to identify why I was weeping. She wanted to know specifically what emotion I felt that led me to cry. She helped me understand that deep inside the grown woman running a NASCAR business was a little girl who was deeply wounded. That little girl, the younger me, was full of emotion that had never been expressed, emotion rooted in the hurts she experienced growing up and had never dealt with. I don't cry much anymore when I think about the painful things in my past. I have let the negative emotions go, which has made room for strength to come in.

One of the benefits of therapy was that it helped me connect with my personal story. Figuring out my story and its impact on my life has helped me be a better person, a better wife, a better mom, and a better leader. It's enabled me to get my priorities in line in ways I hadn't for a long time.

Part of my story included not knowing how to have a healthy marriage. After two divorces, I didn't know if I wanted to marry again, but in early 2010, L. W. Miller asked me for a date. I immediately said to myself, *Now* here's *a man I think I could be interested in.*

One reason I pursued therapy was that I desperately didn't want another failed marriage. I could easily see that I was the common denominator in the two broken marriages, so it made sense that I needed to work on myself. Whatever work needed to be done, I wanted to do.

I don't think I would serve you well if I didn't share with you that therapy puts you in touch with pain and dysfunction you might prefer not to think about. Certain things became worse for me before they got better. The issues I dealt with were very emotional and difficult to work through, but I am *so* glad I did it! I'm happier now than I have ever been, and I feel great about my life.

If you ever begin to wonder if you need help with matters of the heart, pay attention. You may be realizing that you need to deal with some things that are holding you back. I can assure you that issues in your heart do influence every aspect of your life. They can be an unseen negative force that keeps you from fulfilling your potential or realizing your dreams. But help is available, and once you confront and wrestle with internal situations that may be causing you problems, you, too, will be glad you've done it.

FIND YOUR VOICE AND USE IT

As part of my therapy, I realized that I never felt I had a voice while I was growing up and into my adult years. All I had was a persona, which was dominated by the fact that I was Dale Earnhardt Sr.'s daughter. If I tried to speak up for what I needed or how I felt, the people with the power to help didn't listen.

Until I became comfortable with myself, I was uncomfortable talking honestly about who my dad really was. The fact is my dad had a huge heart. He truly did, but he struggled to raise a family. Anytime anyone told me how great my dad was, I would smile and speak words of agreement. But at the same time, the voice in my head would say, *Okay, Person-Who-Never-Met-Him, you really don't know what you're talking about. Maybe he was a great racecar driver and knew how to handle the public and the media, but he wasn't a great dad—and that's what mattered most to me.*

Part of finding my voice has been addressing the incomplete legacy of my dad by saying, without guilt or shame, that while he had many good qualities, he also had some significant faults. Being able to say that is one of the most freeing things I have ever done.

In some ways, the goal of my life has been to find my voice and to believe that I matter, that I am worth caring for, and that my hopes and dreams are important. I had to find my voice as a person before I could use it as a leader. That's my hope for you: no matter how you succeed in business, I long for you to succeed also as a person—a person of significance and value who can speak up for yourself and your needs.

Just as I sometimes function as a cheerleader for our race teams, I'm a cheerleader for you. I want you to win—and win big. I know you can do it, and I hope this book has equipped you for it.

DRIVE YOUR WAY INTO VICTORY LANE

You don't have to be a NASCAR driver or fan to want to win—that drive seems to be embedded in all of us. It's the road to success that is unique to each person. We all have different backgrounds, challenges, motivations, and goals, so what winning looks like for you—and the way you achieve it—might be something entirely different from what it looks like for me.

At JRM we customize our cars based on track conditions, driver preferences, and the knowledge we've gained from previous races. In this section, I'll walk you through creating your own custom setup for success based on your current circumstances, your desires, and your history. I encourage you to take the time to reflect on these questions and write down your answers so that you can refer to them as you pursue your dreams. I want you to win, and I believe this setup will position you to run your race well.

YOUR PAST

Growing up as the daughter of a famous racecar driver shaped the person I've become, both in and out of the office. Similarly, your early years and your family of origin have influenced the person you are today.

To answer the next several questions, think about your childhood and teen years.

- How did your family view the idea of success? In what ways did your family set you up to succeed?
- What values were important in your family? What character qualities did you develop in response to these values?
- What challenges did you and your family face? What character qualities did you develop in the face of these challenges?
- What do you wish had turned out differently?
- Who demonstrated good leadership to you in your youth (your parents, an older sibling or relative, a coach, a pastor, a community figure)? What qualities did they display that you admired?
- What made you happiest? When did you feel the most *you*?

Now, consider the period from your young adult years to the present.

- What life events have shaped your views on success and your ability to achieve it?
- How have your values from childhood been tested as an adult? How has your commitment to those values strengthened or evolved?
- What challenges have affected your adult years? What character qualities have you developed in the face of these challenges?

- What regrets from your adult years do you have?
- Who has demonstrated good leadership to you as an adult (your parents, a professor, a friend, a coworker)? What qualities did they display that you admired?
- What made you happiest? When did you feel the most *you*?

When you review your answers above, what themes emerge? How might these themes influence the kind of person you are today?

Circle three to five words or phrases from your answers that describe the kind of person you want to be as you pursue success, and write them here:

Draw a box around three to five words or phrases from your answers that describe the kind of person you want to avoid being as you go after success, and write them here:

YOUR PRESENT

Let's shift the focus to your current circumstances. You have to know where you are in order to know how to get to where you want to be.

- What roles do you play in your life? Circle all the words that apply to you:
    - Parent
    - Child
    - Spouse
    - Sibling
    - Friend
    - Mentor
    - Community leader
    - Church leader
    - Caretaker
    - Teacher
    - Employee
    - Manager
    - Business leader
    - Entrepreneur
    - Other: _____
- In which roles do you feel like you are already succeeding? Why?
- In which roles do you feel like you are struggling? Why?
- What challenges are you facing?
- What in your life makes you happiest? What makes you feel the most *you*?
- What in your life makes you the most frustrated?

YOUR FUTURE

Now we can start making concrete plans for getting to the winner's circle. Though you may be seeking improvement in several areas of your life at once, pick just one role to focus on for now. (You can repeat this planning for as many roles as you want.) Write that role here: _____.

What specific goals do you want to achieve with respect to this role? If possible, set specific short-term, medium-term, and long-term goals.

Short-term (in the next year):

Medium-term (in the next three years):

Long-term (in the next five years):

———

Let's consider how the nine lessons I've shared throughout this book can apply to your specific situation.

BE AUTHENTIC AND APPROACHABLE

Being authentic means knowing who you are.

- What strengths can you capitalize on as you move forward?
- What limitations may hold you back?
- What weaknesses can you try to improve?
- Revisit the words and phrases you listed when you described the kind of person you want to become. How can you demonstrate these qualities in your day-to-day life?

Being approachable means not letting your quest for success cut you off from the people around you.

- Think about the key people in your life—family, friends, coworkers, community members, and so on. How can you stay in relationship with them as you pursue your goals?

KNOW HOW TO MAKE DECISIONS

I suggest four steps to making quality decisions. Let's walk through them now as we think about what success could look like for you.

- **Step #1: Begin at the end.** What is the end result you want to see? What does "winning" look like for you?
- **Step #2: Get the facts.** What pieces of information are you missing as you set out to achieve your goal? How will you measure your success?

- **Step #3: Access the experts.** Whom can you turn to for advice? Are there people you should avoid because they do not have your best interest at heart?
- **Step #4: Talk to the people the decision affects.** Who are the key stakeholders affected by your pursuit of success?

POSITION FOR SUCCESS

Taking the time to complete this exercise is already positioning you for success, but here are some additional questions to ask as you focus on your goals.

- Keeping in mind your past and present, how are you already positioned for success?
- It's nearly impossible to succeed alone. How can you build a team of supporters who will help you achieve your goals?
- Are you prepared to seek new ideas and approaches to success? Where will you look for these new perspectives?

LET GO TO MOVE FORWARD

We need to let go of the things that do not move us forward.

- What feelings, fears, old ways of thinking, or people might you need to let go of?
- If you let go of these things, what's the worst that could happen?

- If you let go of these things, what's the best that could happen?
- What sacrifices are involved in letting go?
- What might happen if you *don't* let go?

CUSTOMIZE YOUR COMMUNICATION

Clear communication is one of the foundations of success. It strengthens relationships and allows each party to understand the other's needs and expectations.

- Think of the different audiences you will need to communicate with as you go after your goals. How can you customize your conversations with them to maximize your effectiveness?
- When you communicate, do you tend to focus on facts or feelings? What can you do to remind yourself to stick to the facts as you communicate your needs?
- Think of a conflict you have experienced you wish had turned out differently. Reflecting on your own role in the conflict (not on others'!), consider whether you were honest, respectful, and professional as you communicated your perspective. In what areas can you improve?

AIM FOR THE WIN-WIN

You'll feel the most satisfied with your success when it benefits as many people in your life as possible. However, sometimes your goals will come into conflict with others'. Think proactively about how you can navigate these situations so you can negotiate a win-win.

- What goals or needs do you have in common with the key people who are interested in or affected by your success?
- What goals or needs do you have that conflict with those of the key people on your journey to success? How can you bring these competing goals into alignment?

The road to success is a long one, but one way to keep yourself and your team motivated is to take time to recognize victories when they happen.

- How can you celebrate success on the way to your ultimate win? Write down three specific milestones and what you will do to celebrate them.

MANAGE YOUR EMOTIONS

Feelings aren't bad, but poorly managed emotions can become obstacles to success.

- What negative emotions (such as impatience, frustration, fear, sadness, or anger) do you struggle with that could derail your goals? What strategies can you use to counter the effects of these emotions?

- What healthy outlets can you pursue to keep your emotions in check?
- What can you do to stay focused on the positive when you encounter stressful or disappointing events?

BALANCE YOUR WORK WITH YOUR LIFE

Establishing a healthy life-work balance is critical for success because it allows you to pursue your goals while preserving your physical, mental, emotional, spiritual, and relational health.

- What will you need to say no to as you focus on achieving your goals?
- What boundaries do you need to set up so you can keep work at work and home at home?
- How will you navigate situations where the pursuit of your goals conflicts with time with the important people in your life?
- What outside interests can you engage in or develop so that your quest for success doesn't become all-consuming?
- What can you do to encourage others to balance life and work?

LEAD FROM THE HEART

Leading from the heart means showing genuine emotion while maintaining boundaries and professionalism.

- Think of an example of someone you've seen lead from the

heart. This person can be someone you have a personal relationship with or a more public figure. What qualities of theirs can you emulate?

- What can you do to build connections with others? What can you do to show compassion and empathy for their situations?
- How can you "do good on purpose" in your role?

———

Finally, consider the following questions based on what I'd wish I'd known earlier in my life.

- Who could you ask to mentor you as you work toward success?
- Whom in your personal network can you tap for knowledge and support? How can you expand this network in the future?
- Keeping in mind the principles of being authentic and leading with the heart, what does professionalism look like in your role?
- Keeping in mind the principle of establishing a healthy life-work balance, what does a strong work ethic look like for you?
- Implementing change in your life may require the support of a professional counselor, therapist, life coach, or minister. How will you identify the signs that you need this kind of support, and where will you go to find it?

I hope these questions have helped clarify how you, too, can win at work and in life. I'm rooting for you every step of the way. See you in Victory Lane!

ACKNOWLEDGMENTS

Thank you to my mom (in heaven), who always had my back and was my best friend and my number one supporter in life.

Thank you to my dad (in heaven), whose tough love shaped my foundation and whose legacy in motorsports keeps me focused on my role in NASCAR and on continuing that legacy.

Thank you to my stepdad, Willie, who has always been there for me and supported everything I've done, including being my biggest fan when I drove racecars!

Thank you to my children—Karsyn Kingslee, Kennedy Grace, and Wyatt Wayne—who inspire me daily to be the best momma I can be. You've given me purpose and a reason to be the best version of myself, so I can teach and lead you to be the best versions of yourselves. Having the three of you to love is one of my greatest blessings from God.

Thank you to my siblings—Kerry, Dale Jr., Taylor, and Meredith—who each play a different role in my life and make it better through the time we share and the memories we make. I cannot imagine my life without y'all.

Thank you to my best friends in the whole world. You love me for me and not for who anyone else thinks I am. You make me laugh and remind me not to take myself too seriously, and I enjoy our downtime in the very busy life I lead. I can't imagine life without all the years we've spent as besties, and I look forward to growing into old ladies together.

Thank you to Mr. Hendrick, who always has the right words and encouragement for any situation. I am blessed that our families have the history we have as friends and competitors, which has allowed our relationship—both professionally and personally—to blossom into what it is today. You are an excellent business partner but an even better friend and mentor.

Thank you to Joe Mattes, who was the best boss and mentor during my early working years and who today helps me run JRM like it was his own. I am thankful to work alongside you and continue to learn from you each day. JRM would never be as successful as it is without your leadership, tenacity, and skill.

Thank you to Mike and Tony at JRM, who have helped me through the book-writing process after being so involved with Dale's book, and have only wanted the best for me.

Thank you to my JRM family, for whom I work hard every day as your leader to put us in the best possible position to win on and off the track. Thank you for your support and love

Thank you to Mel Berger, Margaret Riley King, and the WME team for making this book possible through your relationships and expertise.

Thank you to Beth Clark for challenging me with questions to complete my thoughts and putting our conversations down on paper so eloquently. You made it a breeze to relate to you from the very beginning, as we started as strangers and finished this book as friends. I am very lucky in that.

Thank you to Debbie Wickwire, who recognized the spark in our first meeting and knew that God had something special in mind for the two of us. Your thoughtfulness, your prayers, and your talents have been amazing through this journey and I am forever grateful to have you in my life from this point forward.

Thank you, Meaghan Porter, whose enthusiasm as a NASCAR and Earnhardt fan was the first thing I loved about you. You have since shown me your talented skills through the editing of this work. You are a rock star.

Thank you to my team at W publishing—Daisy, Denise, Kristen, Kristi, Caren, and Alex. You all make these things happen, make it fun, and keep going forward to put out a great book in the end.

Thank you to Chris Stanford for the photography that makes this cover spectacular. You pushed me out of my comfort zone in front of the camera.

And to my JRM, Earnhardt, and NASCAR fans everywhere, thank you for your loyalty, enthusiasm, and passion for our sport.

NOTES

Chapter 1: My Starting Position

1. Brenda Jackson, personal communication with author, September 23, 2018.
2. For example, see Angus Phillips, "NASCAR's Rough Rider," *Washington Post*, June 14, 1987, https://www.washingtonpost.com/archive/sports/1987/06/14/nascars-rough-rider/66622e9f-bb05-4341-9129-a86221055ff1/.
3. Cathy Earnhardt Watkins, personal communication with author, December 20, 2018.

Chapter 2: Big Sister

1. "Dale Earnhardt Jr: My Sister the Protector," interview by Graham Bensinger, *In Depth with Graham Bensinger*, September 5, 2018, video, https://www.youtube.com/watch?time_continue=2&v=15FjRzhRtlY.
2. "Richard Childress," Richard Childress Racing, https://www.rcrracing.com/richard-childress/.

Chapter 3: Moving On

1. Joe Mattes, personal communication with author, September 25, 2018.

Chapter 4: Then Everything Changed

1. "Earnhardt: 'We Were Never Close' to Deal with DEI," ESPN, May 10, 2007, https://www.espn.com/racing/news/story?id=2866102&seriesId=2.

Chapter 6: Know How to Make Decisions

1. Joe Mattes, personal communication with author, September 25, 2018.
2. Mattes, personal communication.

Chapter 7: Position for Success

1. Mattes, personal communication.
2. "About MBS," Management by Strengths, http://www.strengths.com
   /about-mbs.html.
3. Nick Schwartz, "Dale Earnhardt Jr. Opens Up on His Complicated
   Relationship with His Dad," FTW! Racing, *USA Today*, November 28,
   2018, https://ftw.usatoday.com/2018/11/dale-earnhardt-jr-opens-up
   -on-relationship-with-his-dad.

Chapter 8: Let Go to Move Forward

1. Ann Landers, "Misdemeanor Classification Isn't Tough Enough for
   Domestic Abuse," *Tulsa World*, August 3, 1997, https://www.tulsaworld
   .com/archive/misdemeanor-classification-isn-t-tough-enough-for
   -domestic-abuse/article_ea0656d3-bd7b-55ac-aff6-a1e317ad2310.html.
2. David Newton, "Tony Eury Sr. Out at JR Motorsports," ESPN,
   September 7, 2012, https://www.espn.com/racing/nascar/nationwide
   /story/_/id/8349183/jr-motorsports-parts-ways-tony-eury-sr
3. Newton, "Tony Eury Sr. Out."
4. Joyce Meyer, *Healing the Soul of a Woman* (New York: FaithWords,
   2018), 60.
5. Meyer, 59.
6. Fred Shapiro, "Who Wrote the Serenity Prayer?" *Yale Alumni Magazine*,
   July–August 2008, https://yalealumnimagazine.com/articles/2143.

Chapter 9: Customize Your Communication

1. James Humes, "The Art of Communication Is the Language of
   Leadership," Fresh Business Thinking, March 27, 2008, https://www
   .freshbusinessthinking.com/the-art-of-communication-is-the-language
   -of-leadership/.
2. Though sometimes attributed to Irish playwright George Bernard
   Shaw, this sentiment may have originated from an article by William
   H. Whyte titled "Is Anybody Listening?" that was published in a 1950
   issue of *Fortune*. See https://quoteinvestigator.com/2014/08/31/illusion/.
3. Neil M. Clark, "Spunk Never Cost a Man a Job Worth Having," *American
   Magazine* 111, no. 3 (March 1931): 63.

4. *The Lao Tzu (Tao-te Ching)*, quoted in Wing-tsit Chan, *The Way of Lao Tzu* (n.p.: Revenio Books, 2015), ch. 49, https://books.google.com /books?id=X4L_CwAAQBAJ.

Chapter 11: Manage Your Emotions

1. Joe Mattes, personal communication with the author, September 25, 2018.
2. John Gray, *Men Are from Mars, Women Are from Venus: A Practical Guide to Improving Communication and Getting What You Want in Relationships* (New York: HarperCollins, 1992).
3. Jim McKay, "Opening credits," *The Wide World of Sports*, ABC.

Chapter 12: Balance Your Work with Your Life

1. Ashley Stahl, "The Importance of Work-Life Balance—And How to Achieve It," *Forbes*, October 22, 2018, https://www.forbes.com/sites /ashleystahl/2018/10/22/the-importance-of-work-life-balance-and -how-to-achieve-it/#37053aac4e05.
2. Ryan Jenkins, "This Is Why Millennials Care So Much About Work-Life Balance," LinkedIn, July 13, 2018, https://www.linkedin.com /pulse/why-millennials-care-so-much-work-life-balance-ryan-jenkins.

Chapter 13: Lead from the Heart

1. *Blue Bloods*, season 9, episode 7, "By Hook or by Crook," directed by David M. Barret, written by Siobhan Byrne O'Connor, aired November 9, 2018, on CBS.
2. "From Dale Jr.," The Dale Jr. Foundation, https://www.thedalejrfoundation .org/about/default.aspx.

Chapter 14: Preparing for Your Race

1. Stephen R. Covey, *The Seven Habits of Highly Effective People* (New York: Simon & Schuster, 1989), 161.
2. Myles Munroe, *Myles Munroe Devotional & Journal: 365 Days to Realize Your Potential* (Shippensburg, PA: Destiny House, 2007), week 38, day 4.
3. Kathy Caprino, "How to Find a Great Mentor—First, Don't Ever Ask a Stranger," *Forbes*, September 21, 2014, https://www.forbes.com/sites/kathy caprino/2014/09/21/how-to-find-a-great-mentor-first-dont-ever-ask-a -stranger/#4f8ba8f1dfa1.

ABOUT THE AUTHOR

Kelley Earnhardt Miller is part owner and general manager of JR Motorsports and is considered one of the most prominent businesswomen in NASCAR today. She oversees the company's race team, management team, and business ventures for her brother, Dale Earnhardt Jr. The daughter of seven-time NASCAR champion Dale Earnhardt, Earnhardt Miller graduated from the University of North Carolina at Charlotte with a bachelor of arts in business administration. A multiple-award recipient, in 2015 she was named one of *Sports Business Journal*'s Game Changers / Women in Sports Business for her impact on the motorsports industry. Kelley is married to L. W. Miller and is mom to Karsyn, Kennedy, and Wyatt.